PREPARING FOR PRACTICE

Second Edition

PREPARING FOR PRACTICE

Legal Analysis and Writing in Law School's First Year

Second Edition

Amy Vorenberg
Professor Emeritus
University of New Hampshire Franklin Pierce School of Law

Jennifer Davis
Professor of Legal Skills
University of Massachusetts School of Law

Anna Elbroch
Clinical Assistant Professor and Director of Legal Writing
University of New Hampshire Franklin Pierce School of Law

ASPEN PUBLISHING

To contact Customer Service, e-mail customer.service@aspenpublishing.com, call 1-800-950-5259, or mail correspondence to:

Aspen Publishing
Attn: Order Department
1 Wall Street
Burlington, MA 01803

Cover image: Song_about_summer/Shutterstock.com

Printed in the United States of America.

1 2 3 4 5 6 7 8 9 0

ISBN 978-1-5438-0928-2

Library of Congress Cataloging-in-Publication Data

Names: Vorenberg, Amy, author. | Davis, Jennifer, author. | Elbroch, Anna, author.
Title: Preparing for practice : legal analysis and writing in law school's first year / Jennifer Davis, Professor of Legal Skills, University of Massachusetts School of Law; Anna Elbroch, Clinical Assistant Professor and Director of Legal Writing, University of New Hampshire Franklin Pierce School of Law; Amy Vorenberg, Professor Emeritus University of New Hampshire Franklin Pierce School of Law.
Description: Second Edition. | Burlington : Aspen Publishing, 2024. | Includes index. | Summary: "Legal Writing primer for first-year law school students"-- Provided by publisher.
Identifiers: LCCN 2023059780 | ISBN 9781543809282 (hardcover) | ISBN 9781543809282 (ebook)
Subjects: LCSH: Legal composition. | Legal research--United States. | Practice of law--United States. | LCGFT: Textbooks
Classification: LCC KF250 .V67 2024 | DDC 808.06/634--dc23
LC record available at https://lccn.loc.gov/2023059780

SUSTAINABLE FORESTRY INITIATIVE
Certified Chain of Custody
At Least 10% Certified Forest Content
www.sfiprogram.org
SFI-01028

About Aspen Publishing

Aspen Publishing is a leading provider of educational content and digital learning solutions to law schools in the U.S. and around the world. Aspen provides best-in-class solutions for legal education through authoritative textbooks, written by renowned authors, and breakthrough products such as Connected eBooks, Connected Quizzing, and PracticePerfect.

The Aspen Casebook Series (famously known among law faculty and students as the "red and black" casebooks) encompasses hundreds of highly regarded textbooks in more than eighty disciplines, from large enrollment courses, such as Torts and Contracts to emerging electives such as Sustainability and the Law of Policing. Study aids such as the *Examples & Explanations* and the *Emanuel Law Outlines* series, both highly popular collections, help law students master complex subject matter.

Major products, programs, and initiatives include:

- **Connected eBooks** are enhanced digital textbooks and study aids that come with a suite of online content and learning tools designed to maximize student success. Designed in collaboration with hundreds of faculty and students, the Connected eBook is a significant leap forward in the legal education learning tools available to students.
- **Connected Quizzing** is an easy-to-use formative assessment tool that tests law students' understanding and provides timely feedback to improve learning outcomes. Delivered through CasebookConnect.com, the learning platform already used by students to access their Aspen casebooks, Connected Quizzing is simple to implement and integrates seamlessly with law school course curricula.
- **PracticePerfect** is a visually engaging, interactive study aid to explain commonly encountered legal doctrines through easy-to-understand animated videos, illustrative examples, and numerous practice questions. Developed by a team of experts, PracticePerfect is the ideal study companion for today's law students.
- The **Aspen Learning Library** enables law schools to provide their students with access to the most popular study aids on the market across all of their courses. Available through an annual subscription, the online library consists of study aids in e-book, audio, and video formats with full text search, note-taking, and highlighting capabilities.
- Aspen's **Digital Bookshelf** is an institutional-level online education bookshelf, consolidating everything students and professors need to ensure success. This program ensures that every student has access to affordable course materials from day one.
- **Leading Edge** is a community centered on thinking differently about legal education and putting those thoughts into actionable strategies. At the core of the program is the Leading Edge Conference, an annual gathering of legal education thought leaders looking to pool ideas and identify promising directions of exploration.

To our students

About the Authors

Amy Vorenberg, J.D., is an expert in criminal and sexual violence law and legal analysis. She began her legal career working as a prosecutor in the office of the Manhattan District Attorney and then as an Assistant Attorney General in New Hampshire. She then moved to the New Hampshire Public Defender's office where she started a criminal clinic in partnership with the University of New Hampshire Franklin Pierce School of Law where she ultimately joined the faculty and taught for over 20 years. Vorenberg taught Criminal Law and was the Director of the School's Legal Writing faculty. She has authored or co-authored law review articles and several books, including *Preparing for Practice: Legal Analysis and Writing in Law School's First Year (First Edition), Series A, B, and C.*

Jennifer Davis is currently a Professor of Legal Skills at the University of Massachusetts School of Law where she teaches legal writing and analysis to first-year J.D. students. Before joining UMass Law, Professor Davis taught legal writing to J.D. students at the University of New Hampshire Franklin Pierce School of Law and Suffolk University School of Law. She also served as Director of Graduate Skills at UNH Law, teaching legal analysis and writing to international students. Professor Davis graduated from Suffolk University School of Law and clerked for judges of the Maine Superior Court and the Juvenile Court of Massachusetts. She also worked as an appellate attorney in the Suffolk County District Attorney's Office and argued cases before the Massachusetts Supreme Judicial Court and Massachusetts Appeals Court.

Anna Elbroch practiced for 16 years prior to teaching. Her practice included indigent criminal defense at New Hampshire Public Defender, and representation of children in private practice in New Hampshire in a variety of proceedings including child protection, marital, special education, and delinquency cases. Anna is the Director of Legal Writing at University of New Hampshire Franklin Pierce School of Law where she focuses on practical skill-building, online education, legal writing and research, and teaching.

Summary of Contents

Contents   xiii
Acknowledgments   xvii

CHAPTER 1   Learning a New Language   1
CHAPTER 2   Overview of Predictive Legal Analysis   5
CHAPTER 3   Where Does the Law We Use Come From?   13
CHAPTER 4   How We Use the Law: Hierarchy of Law   23
CHAPTER 5   Sample Case File   31
CHAPTER 6   How to Read, Understand, and Brief Statutes and Cases   43
CHAPTER 7   Synthesizing Rules and Identifying Decisive Facts   65
CHAPTER 8   Overview of the Office Memorandum   75
CHAPTER 9   Writing the Discussion Section of an Interoffice
              Memorandum   89
CHAPTER 10   Advanced Writing: Multi-Issue Analysis   113
CHAPTER 11   Counter-Analysis   125
CHAPTER 12   Client Letters and Emails   131
CHAPTER 13   Revising   139
CHAPTER 14   Legal Writing and ChatGPT   147

Appendix A   Examples of Different Types of Legal Writing   151
Appendix B   Additional Example of a Predictive Legal Memorandum   163
Appendix C   Case Brief for Winstead   169
Appendix D   Magnolia Cases on Defintion of "Way"   173
Appendix E   Additional Outline Example   181
Index   183

Contents

Acknowledgments   *xvii*

CHAPTER 1   **Learning a New Language**   **1**

Introduction   1
What to Expect in Your Legal Writing Class   2
Citation? I Have to Learn That Too?   3
What Do I Need to Do to Succeed at Legal Writing?   3
How This Textbook is Organized   4

CHAPTER 2   **Overview of Predictive Legal Analysis**   **5**

Introduction   5
Predictive Legal Analysis and Writing   7

CHAPTER 3   **Where Does the Law We Use Come From?**   **13**

The U.S. Constitution and Federalism   14
The Three Branches of Government   15
    The Legislative Branch   15
    The Executive Branch   15
    The Judicial Branch   17

CHAPTER 4   **How We Use the Law: Hierarchy of Law**   **23**

Introduction   23
Hierarchy of Law   24

CHAPTER 5   **Sample Case File**   **31**

Introduction   31

CHAPTER 6   **How to Read, Understand, and Brief
Statutes and Cases**   **43**

Introduction   43
Reading and Understanding a Statute   44
How Do Courts Interpret Statutes?   47
Reading and Understanding Cases   48
    Why Brief Cases?   49
Studying a Case   53
    Breaking Down a Case   53
    Identifying Parts of a Case: Citation, Caption, Date,
    Summary, and Headnotes   53
    The Procedural History   56
    Distinguishing Background Case Facts Versus
    Decisive Case Facts   56
    Identifying the Court's Reasoning (IRAC) 58
    Understanding How a Court Reasons   60

CHAPTER 7   **Synthesizing Rules and Identifying
Decisive Facts**   **65**

Introduction   65
    Identifying Decisive Facts in a Client's Case 70
    Synthesizing a Rule in Mr. Clover's Case 70
    The Synthesized Rule in Mr. Clover's Case 73
Identifying Client Facts   73

CHAPTER 8   **Overview of the Office Memorandum**   **75**

Introduction   75
Sample Memorandum   76
Suggested Memorandum Drafting Order   80
Breakdown of the Parts of an Interoffice
Legal Memorandum   80
    The Heading   81
    The Issue or Question Presented   81
    The Brief Answer or Summary   84
    The Facts   85
    The Discussion Section   87
    The Conclusion   87

CHAPTER 9   **Writing the Discussion Section of an Interoffice Memorandum**   **89**

Introduction   89
How to Organize the Information   90
   Make an Outline   91
Step-by-Step Approach to Making an Outline   92
Explaining the Law in a Discussion   96
   The Roadmap (aka Global) Paragraph   97
   Explaining the Law Using Case Examples   99
   A Step-by-Step Approach to Writing the
      Explanation of the Law   100
Applying the Law in a Discussion   104
Organization: Internal Paragraph Structure   109
   Writing the Paragraph's First Sentence   110
   Using Parallel Structure   111

CHAPTER 10   **Advanced Writing: Multi-Issue Analysis**   **113**

Introduction   113
   Developing the Rules in a Multi-Issue Analysis   114

CHAPTER 11   **Counter-Analysis**   **125**

Introduction   125
Fact and Law-Based Counter-Analysis   126
Where Does a Counter-Analysis Go in a Memo?   129

CHAPTER 12   **Client Letters and Emails**   **131**

Introduction   131
Client Letters and Emails   131
   Organization—Long Form   131
   Organization—Short Form   133
   Style and Format   135
Tips on Professional Email Communication   135

CHAPTER 13   **Revising**   **139**

Introduction   139
Large-Scale Revising   140
Internal Paragraph Revising   141
Micro Revising: Grammar and Mechanics   141

CHAPTER 14   Legal Writing and ChatGPT   147

Introduction   147
Law School Policies on ChatGPT   147
Research   148
Ethics   148
Bias   149

Appendix A   *Examples of Different Types of Legal Writing*   *151*
Appendix B   *Additional Example of a Predictive Legal Memorandum*   *163*
Appendix C   *Case Brief for* Winstead   *169*
Appendix D   *Magnolia Cases on Defintion of "Way"*   *173*
Appendix E   *Additional Outline Example*   *181*
Index   *183*

Acknowledgments

Thank you to all UNH School of Law Legal Writing professors, past and present, who have read, tweaked, discussed, and reworked case files over the years. Thank you to UNH research assistants Lea Polito, Tristan Meyer, Taylor Vitti, Sommer Skeps, and Keirsten Schwanbeck, who contributed with case charts, casefile drafts, and ideas. Being a legal writing professor requires teamwork, and we acknowledge and appreciate all members of our teams at UNH Law and UMass Law, including professors, administrators, teaching assistants, administrative assistants, and colleagues.

PREPARING FOR PRACTICE

Second Edition

CHAPTER 1

Learning a New Language

INTRODUCTION

You have arrived at law school with solid writing skills. After all, you would not be here without them. Legal writing, however, requires some unique skills. In many ways, learning legal writing is more like learning a new language. It is important to remember this because there will be times when you will say to yourself, "I thought I was a good writer. I did well in under-grad." Or "I write for work all the time and get good feedback." When these moments hit, remind yourself that legal writing is a new genre to which you are not yet accustomed.

First, in legal writing, less is more. Good legal writing means getting to the point quickly. This usually means that legal writers start with their conclusion, so that legal readers understand where the writer is headed. It also means that legal writers use short sentences and manageable paragraphs, so the legal reader moves easily through the writing. If you are a political science major or a student of humanities, this style may seem backward to you. Legal writing is focused on the reader, whereas academic writing is a product that reflects self-discovery. In legal writing, when drafting legal documents, you are always asked to put yourself in the place of the reader.

Second, in many law practices, time is money. Written communication must therefore be done in the most expedient manner possible. Whether you are writing a letter to a client or an email to a colleague in your office or cor-responding with an opposing counsel, you will likely be mindful that the time you spend researching and writing will cost the client money. The challenge is never to sacrifice quality and accuracy for expedience or to jeopardize your professional responsibilities by not properly using an online tool.

Third, long gone are the days of "heretofore" and the "party-of-the-first-part." Effective legal writing is constructed with attention to plain English. Writing like a lawyer means using language and structure that a client can understand. Colleagues and judges may understand the legal lingo better than a client, but they do not have the time or the patience to decipher complex words and dense paragraphs.

Finally, and perhaps most importantly, legal writing is a bit of a mischaracterization. You are learning how to analyze the law and communicate about it effectively. That means that you must study and understand the law before you learn how to write effectively. Your legal writing class is about analyzing as much as it is about writing.

Consider yourself a student of a new language and a new way of communicating. Do not despair if your excellence in writing before law school does not translate automatically into excellence in your first semester of law school. Be patient, and you will soon see that, with guidance, your skills are indeed transferable to legal writing.

WHAT TO EXPECT IN YOUR LEGAL WRITING CLASS

You will probably notice that your legal writing class does not look like your other first-year classes. Your legal writing class will be smaller. The book will be different, as it will likely be shorter and organized more like a reference book or a textbook, as opposed to a case book. The syllabus may look different. You will notice that you have more assignments due and that the course information for the class contains requisites for formatting, rubrics, or professionalism.

The first-year legal writing class is the first time you will get to act like a lawyer. In legal writing, you learn law in the context of a hypothetical client's problem. You will communicate your analysis of the problem and solution in written documents. If you were in medical school, this class would be the first "clinical" course, in which you learn the basics of assessing a patient by interviewing and examining a mock patient.

Also, you and your professor share the same goal—your success as a legal writer. To help you achieve that goal, your professor will provide feedback on your writing. Perhaps for the first time in your life, you will receive detailed input about analysis, organization, grammar, and style. At first, this may come as a shock, but the feedback will teach you to transfer those solid writing skills you brought to law school into effective legal writing. While you might wince a little (or a lot) when you receive feedback from your professor, the feedback given is not personal. Its only purpose is to help you become an excellent lawyer. If you strive to maintain a growth mindset—that you can learn and adapt to the challenges you face in law school—and approach the feedback from this perspective, you will grow and learn as a student.

In addition, in your legal writing class, you will likely receive feedback from peers and certainly give and receive feedback throughout your career as an attorney. No one expects you to master legal writing the first time you try it. Writing is a skill that develops and improves over time, no matter how long you have pursued it. Engage with the process and focus as best you can on learning rather than beating yourself up for any missteps.

You could be in a legal office next summer or a clinic or residency in the coming year. Your professor's goal is to prepare you for that experience. Use your professor's expertise. Risk missteps. Work through the difficult learning process to communicate your analysis effectively in writing. Being open to critique and being willing to work with your professor will help you get the most out of your legal writing class and better prepare you for when you are in the "real" world.

CITATION? I HAVE TO LEARN THAT TOO?

You will notice that the cases you read for your other first-year classes rely on many kinds of authority, including other cases, statutes, and secondary sources, which are sources that comment upon and explain the law. Judges and lawyers use a uniform system of legal citation so that readers can easily find the authorities relied upon in documents and to efficiently show the reader the weight and persuasiveness of the authority. Very particular rules govern this citation system. You will use the *Bluebook*, the *ALWD Citation Manual*, or *The Indigo Book*, an open-source online, to cite accurately. Use the citation manual required by your legal writing professor. You will likely use these sources during and after law school, so hold on to them! When you refer to cases, statutes, or other authorities in your legal writing, you will use the same uniform system and a citation resource as a reference. At first, the citation rules will seem mysterious and very persnickety. With practice, you will get used to the rules, and how to cite will become second nature to you.

A quick way to undermine a legal reader's confidence in your argument is to ignore details like citation. After all, if a judge cannot rely on your ability to accurately state where information comes from in the law, then the judge will reasonably question the accuracy of what you are saying. As a result, one key thing you can do to become an effective and credible attorney is to understand how to correctly indicate where information comes from in a statute or case. Again, be patient with yourself, and you will learn to cite accurately.

WHAT DO I NEED TO DO TO SUCCEED AT LEGAL WRITING?

The phrase legal writing professors hear repeatedly during the first weeks of the semester is, "I can't believe how much time it takes to write a short memo!" Thus, the Number One piece of advice is: Do not underestimate the time it takes to complete an assignment. While waiting until the last minute may have worked in college, it is unlikely to work in law school. Even a mere three-page assignment can take much longer to complete than you think it will.

The way to succeed in legal writing is as follows:

- Start early and plan ahead.
- Read the directions—know what is being asked.
- Learn to *study* (not just read) the law.
- Plan your writing with outlining or other strategies before you start drafting.
- Meet with your professor and your teaching assistant to ask questions.
- Revise.
- Revise.
- Revise again.

Because learning about legal writing is like learning a new language, it will help if you are willing to make mistakes and learn from them. Becoming an effective legal analyst and writer is a **recursive** process. With each new assignment, you will have a chance to practice a skill you have already tried and to learn new ones. Stay open to retrying, rethinking, and revising!

HOW THIS TEXTBOOK IS ORGANIZED

We use a sample case file throughout this text, *State v. Cleo Clover*. The case file contains the information you need to solve the client's problem. This includes:

- A memorandum from a supervising attorney that explains the facts of the client's problem
- Five cases from a fictional jurisdiction (Magnolia)
- A statute from the same fictional jurisdiction (Magnolia)

You will also find several examples of memos, including a sample of what the finished product could look like in *State v. Clover*. Use these examples to determine conventions in legal writing. Not every legal memo will look the same, but the memos will follow particular trends, such as explaining the law before applying it to your client's factual scenario. The next few chapters will break down some of those legal writing conventions, how our legal system is structured, and the various sources of law. The rest of this book will focus on the parts of the sample case file, the writing process, and other forms of lawyer communication.

Overview of Predictive Legal Analysis

INTRODUCTION

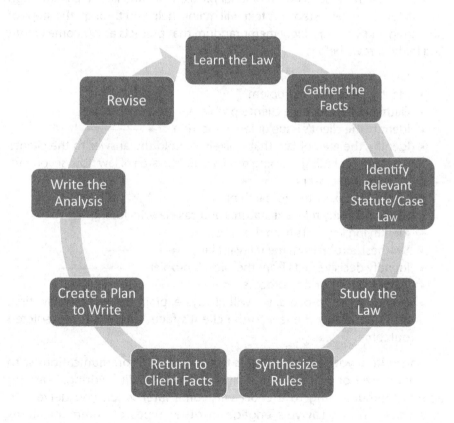

Lawyers are problem solvers. Clients come to lawyers with a set of facts that typically present a legal question. The question might involve a specialized area of law such as criminal law, business law, civil rights law, family law, municipal law, or environmental law. Or it might involve a combination of multiple areas of law.

Lawyers gather their clients' facts and then research law to identify how the law might apply to the facts and provide a solution to the client's problem or an answer to the client's question. Communicating the solution to a client or court is often done in writing—memoranda and other forms of legal writing. The process of legal writing, illustrated on the previous page, is reiterative. It requires gathering facts, researching the law, analyzing the law, honing in on the decisive client's facts, finding answers and solutions, and communicating those answers and solutions. Other law school courses and texts will teach how to gather clients' facts and research law. This textbook will show you how to **analyze** the law and **explain** the answers in writing.

Below is a more detailed list of legal problem-solving key steps. Although we will touch on each step, this text will mainly help you through the steps of preparing and writing a legal memorandum that predicts an outcome identified in the arrows below.

- Learn the law.
- Meet a client with a problem.
- Gather facts about the client's problem.
- Identify the client's issue or legal question. ◄──────────
- Identify the area of law that is likely to hold the answer to the client's question, including learning more about the area of law from secondary sources, if necessary.
- Create and execute a research plan.
- Read and study relevant statutes and case law, including ◄────── identifying key facts from the case law.
- Synthesize rules from the relevant law. ◄──────
- Identify decisive facts from the client's problem. ◄──────
- Complete the writing process. ◄──────
- In the writing process, we will always explain the relevant law first, and then apply the law to the client's facts to support a predicted outcome.

The writing you will learn in this text focuses on communications with another lawyer or a client—what lawyers call *predictive* writing. Learning about communicating to a court will come later when you delve into *persuasive* writing. Lawyers engage in other types of communications and documents, including explaining a law or legal principle unrelated to a client's problem. We've included examples of these variations in the Appendix.

PREDICTIVE LEGAL ANALYSIS AND WRITING

Predictive legal analysis and writing educate the reader on the relevant law and how the relevant law applies specifically to the client's circumstances. The analysis, typically written in **legal memorandum** form, should be thorough enough and provide sufficient support so that the reader understands the likely outcome of the legal issue, and any potential counter-analysis and how that might be addressed. A legal memo typically follows a set structure. It starts with a recitation of the Issue posing the legal question, followed by a Brief Answer to that question. Then, a facts section and the legal analysis or Discussion come next. The Discussion is where you explain and apply the law relevant to the legal issue.

Here is how a request for a predictive analysis and legal memorandum might unfold in practice.

Imagine that you have completed your first year of law school. You have an internship or a paid job with a firm. One of your new colleagues, perhaps your supervisor, asks you to find out the answer to a legal question that pertains to a client's case. She asks you to draft a memo that sets out the law on the particular question and also how the law might affect the client's situation.

You learn that one of her clients, whom she represents primarily on business matters, has been accused of shoplifting. It turns out that the client has had similar trouble before. The lawyer is preparing to defend the client. She wants to know if evidence of the client's prior misdeeds will be relevant (and thus potentially admissible) in the client's trial. She asks that you research and advise her on whether the evidence is legally relevant under state law.

First, you read the client's file (or whatever documents your supervisor gave you), and then you research the issue. Once you have a good idea of the law, you draft a legal memorandum.

What follows is an example of the predictive analysis you might return to her. The annotations highlight some of the broad legal conventions you will employ in your legal writing.

> Legal memorandums can be their own documents or in e-mail form. If an e-memo, the structure will change. We discuss the e-memo structure in Chapter 12.

MEMORANDUM

To: Attorney Supervisor
From: Student Lawyer
Date: September 15, 20XX
Re: *State v. Albert:* Criminal Theft—Relevance of Albert's prior shoplifting, #CR23456

Issue

The question is presented in the context of the client's case.

In Maureen Albert's trial for theft of a ham from a Hannaford Supermarket (*Hannaford*), is evidence of a prior incident relevant where in the prior case, Albert removed a turkey from the same Hannaford without paying?

Brief Answer

The Brief Answer directly and efficiently answers the question posed in the Issue.

Probably yes. Evidence of Albert's earlier shoplifting incident is probably relevant under the New Hampshire Rule of Evidence 404(b). Admission of prior bad act evidence under Rule 404(b) requires that: (1) the evidence is relevant for a purpose other than showing the defendant's character, (2) there is clear proof that the defendant committed the prior act, and (3) the probative value of the evidence outweighs its prejudicial impact. As instructed, this memo addresses only the question of relevance. Albert has made her intent an issue by specifically claiming she removed the ham accidentally. The evidence of Albert's prior shoplifting is thus likely relevant to rebut her claim that she took the ham by accident.

Facts

The facts are written objectively; they are stated without trying to convince the reader of any particular outcome.

In November 2011, three months before the current incident occurred, Maureen Albert left the Hannaford's in Concord, New Hampshire, without paying for a turkey she had placed in the bottom of her cart. Albert returned the turkey, was warned about her behavior, and was not prosecuted.

In February 2012, Albert took a cart containing a spiral ham out of the same Hannaford's without paying for it. When a Hannaford's employee stopped her in the parking lot, Albert said she left the store because she had forgotten her wallet in her car. She stated that she did not intend to steal the ham and had removed it from the store accidentally.

The State charged Albert with shoplifting for the second incident. In her trial, the State wants to introduce evidence of the turkey incident to prove that Albert intended to steal the ham.

Discussion

The Discussion or the legal analysis will always explain the law before it is applied to the client facts.

Albert's prior act involving the turkey is likely relevant for a purpose other than character because she raised the issue of intent, and the prior act is factually similar and close in time to the charged act. Evidence is relevant for a purpose other than character (1) if it has a direct bearing on an issue actually in dispute, and (2) if a clear and logical connection exists between that act and the crime charged. *State v. McGlew*, 658 A.2d 1191, 1194 (N.H. 1995). The trial court must make specific findings on each element. *Id.*

When there is more than one ~~issue~~ *element, headings can help guide the reader.*

1. Direct Bearing on Issue in Dispute

This paragraph explains the part of the law described in the heading.

Evidence of a prior act is relevant to refute a defendant's claim that the crime was committed by accident. *State v. Lesnick*, 677 A.2d 686, 690 (N.H. 1996). For example, the court in *Lesnick* admitted evidence of a prior act because it was relevant to show the absence of an accident where the defendant claimed she had stabbed her husband in self-defense because she believed him to be an unknown intruder. *Id.* In contrast, the court excluded the evidence where the defendant denied involvement in the crime, specifically that she had not injured a child in her care. *State v. Blackey*, 623 A.2d 1333, 1334 (N.H. 1993). The court reasoned that the prior evidence of child abuse was irrelevant because, by denying the current crime altogether, the defendant had not placed her intent or propensity at issue. *Id.* at 1334; *State v. Whittaker*, 642 A.2d 936, 938 (N.H. 1994).

Albert's prior act is likely relevant here because she claims she took the ham by accident. Like the defendant in *Lesnick*, who admitted the stabbing but claimed it was an accident, Albert made her intent an issue by claiming she took the ham unintentionally. Evidence of a prior similar act is relevant to disproving Albert's claim of accident. This is in contrast to a claim that she denied involvement in taking the ham, like in *Blackey*, where the prior evidence was inadmissible because the defendant denied involvement in the accused crime. Because the evidence of the prior act is offered for a purpose other than Albert's character or propensity to steal meat, it is probably admissible.

This paragraph applies the law just explained in the paragraph above to the client facts.

2. Clear and Logical Connection

Next, the evidence probably meets the second prong of the relevancy analysis because a clear, logical connection exists between the charged act of stealing a ham and the prior act of taking a turkey. A clear, logical connection exists where the acts are factually similar, and the prior act is "not so remote in time as to eliminate the nexus" between the prior act and the crime charged. *McGlew*, 658 A.2d at 1194. The State must articulate a precise chain of reasoning between the prior act and the charged act without relying on inferences about the defendant's character, which are forbidden. *Id.* at 1195. For example, in *Lesnick*, a logical connection existed between the prior stabbing and the charged stabbing because the defendant committed each crime under similar emotional circumstances against the same victim using the same weapon. *Id.* The factual similarities between the two acts permitted the conclusion that the defendant intended the second act since two identical "accidents" within a few months were unlikely. *Id.*

This paragraph and the next explain another part of the law.

Where two acts are significantly different, the court will not admit evidence of the first to prove the defendant's intent in committing the second act. *McGlew*, 658 A.2d at 1194. In *McGlew* the State failed to establish a nexus between a prior accusation of sexual molestation and the charged act of sexual assault because the prior act, which occurred six years earlier, involved a victim of a different age and gender and a different sex act. *Id.* The factual differences between the two acts suggested that the defendant might have had differing intent during each. *See id.* (noting that the prior act was not relevant, although intent was an element of the charge).

Here, Albert removed the turkey and the ham, similar products, from the same store, using the same method of removal—all facts that show that the second incident was not an accident. Like *Lesnick*, where the close factual similarity between the prior act and the charged act made the prior act relevant to the defendant's intent, here, the virtually identical facts probably make Albert's prior act relevant to her subsequent taking of the turkey.

This paragraph and the next apply the law just explained to the client facts to support your predicted outcome.

Moreover, the close time frame between Albert's two incidents further strengthens their connection. The closer the temporal proximity between two acts, the more likely a court is to find that the actor had the same intent at both times. *See Lesnick*,

677 A.2d at 690 (emphasizing the temporal proximity of the charged and prior acts). In *Lesnick*, the prior act was relevant because it occurred only two months before the charged crime, whereas, in *McGlew*, the prior crime was not admitted, in part. After all, it occurred six years earlier. Similar to Lesnick, who committed the two acts within two months, Albert committed the two acts within three months. Although a person may make one mistake, she is unlikely to make two identical mistakes within a few months. The short time between Albert's two acts supports their logical connection. Because the prior act demonstrates Albert's intent, the court probably will find that the evidence meets the relevancy requirement of the three-part test.

In this paragraph, the writer addresses a counter point. Still, the law is explained before it is applied to the client facts.

Albert's only argument in her favor likely relies on the underlying purpose of 404(b). She could argue that allowing the bad act evidence against her goes against the purpose behind 404(b) and its limitations. *Id.* at 1195 (holding purpose underlying rule 404(b) is to ensure that a defendant is tried on the merits of the case and not on character). However, the concern that a defendant is not convicted based on character is met where, as here, there is a sufficient, specific purpose for its admission. By claiming that she mistakenly took the turkey, Albert placed her own intent to commit theft at issue. The prosecutor would probably be successful in arguing that the purpose of the evidence is to refute that claim and not to demonstrate her bad character.

Notice that the memorandum is an informative document that explains the law before it applies the law to the client's facts to predict that the prior evidence will come in as evidence in a trial against the client. The memorandum also includes a short counter-analysis at the end. This tells the reader that you have considered the opposing arguments and legal analysis. It also gives the reader a full picture of the legal issue. Remember that the memorandum is supposed to be a thorough and accurate analysis so that your supervisor can decide the best course of action; therefore, any weaknesses in the case must be addressed. The information provided in the memo will be critical to your supervisor, who will use it to advise the client on whether to take a plea in the case or go to trial.

 **Video Quiz**

CHAPTER 3

Where Does the Law We Use Come From?

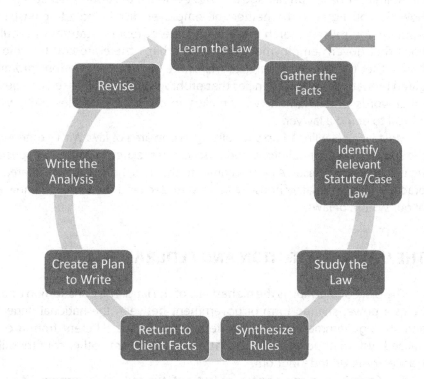

We begin our problem-solving, recursive process by learning the law. Legal problem-solving requires executing a research plan that will lead you to the law applicable to your client's problem. Learning to write effectively as a lawyer means you will need to be a good and careful analyzer of the law. First, we need to review where the law comes from. In the United States, law comes from many sources, and this chapter will review those sources.

You will notice that in your law school courses many of the cases you read are appellate opinions. Appellate opinions come from courts that review the decisions of lower courts and other adjudicatory bodies. Appellate opinions make good vehicles for learning law because they often summarize and apply important legal concepts.

The appellate opinions you read are often the last chapter of a legal issue that begins with a client's problem. The case probably started where most cases start: when a client goes to see a lawyer for help. Clients come in all shapes and sizes, including individuals, corporations, state agencies, and non-profit organizations. When a client comes to a lawyer, they are typically looking to solve a problem or answer a question. The first step for the lawyer in answering the client's question is to figure out what laws will determine the solutions or answers.

Let's say a 60-year-old woman comes to a lawyer because she has been fired and thinks her employer was wrong. She suspects she is being discriminated against based on her age and has evidence to support her suspicion. How do you figure out whether the employer discriminated against the woman? You must research if there are state or federal statutes or regulations that govern employment matters. Perhaps there are court opinions from either the state or federal courts. There might be regulations promulgated by state or federal agencies that prohibit termination based on age. In other words, understanding what makes up our system of rules and laws is critical to being a lawyer.

Most lawyers will end up specializing in one area of law. With experience, the statutes, cases, regulations, and practices in the area in which you specialize will become familiar. As a newcomer to the field, no matter which area of practice you eventually choose, you must understand the overall framework of our system of laws.

THE U.S. CONSTITUTION AND FEDERALISM

The U.S. Constitution is the highest law of the land. The Constitution establishes a power-sharing form of government between the national (federal) and state governments, known as federalism. This is different from a centralized system of power, such as that practiced in some other countries like France or the United Kingdom.

The Constitution enumerates, or lays out, the federal government's powers; the Tenth Amendment to the U.S. Constitution reserves powers that do not belong to the federal government to the state governments. The states are supreme in matters reserved to them, although there are few powers expressly reserved to states. For matters reserved to the states, such as establishing local governments or regulating intrastate commerce, each state is sovereign and eligible to make and interpret its own laws without any interference from other states and the federal government. As a result, each of the 50 states has its own constitution, statutes, and other sources of law.

All state constitution provisions must comply with the U.S. Constitution and federal statutory law. For instance, a state constitution cannot deny an accused criminal the right to a jury trial because the U.S. Constitution would prohibit such a law. However, State constitutions can provide more protections to individuals than the U.S. Constitution. In general, the Supremacy Clause of the U.S. Constitution provides that federal law is superior to state law. If a state enacts a law that conflicts with federal law, the state law will be preempted, and federal law will govern. What follows is a brief review of civics (for purposes of background and foundation) and a general summary of how the government is structured and the sources of law in the United States.

THE THREE BRANCHES OF GOVERNMENT

There are three branches of government in the United States: the legislative, the executive, and the judicial. All three branches make law. Every state has the same structure, with three branches making laws.

THE LEGISLATIVE BRANCH

The U.S. Constitution gives Congress (made up of the House of Representatives and the Senate) enumerated powers to make laws. Article I of the Constitution specifies the matters on which Congress is allowed to legislate. Congress can only make laws relating to matters listed in Article I. Similarly, state constitutions give state legislatures the power to enact laws.

Congress and state legislatures pass laws called statutes. Statutes start as bills. Then, the state or federal legislature enacts and publishes them. In the federal government, bills are first published as slip laws. At both the federal and state levels, enacted laws are compiled into session laws. Session laws are later incorporated into federal and state statutory codes organized by topic. Federal statutory code compilations include the United States Code (U.S.C.), United States Code Annotated (U.S.C.A.), and United States Code Service (U.S.C.S.). Like the federal government, each state legislature has its own system for codifying statutes and making them accessible to the public.

In Chapter 5 you will read the Magnolia Driving Under the Influence statute. That's an example of a codified state statute.

THE EXECUTIVE BRANCH

The Federal and State Executive

Article II of the U.S. Constitution and each state constitution vests power to execute and enforce laws in the President of the United States or the state governor, respectively. The President or governor carries out these duties with the help of administrative agencies that issue regulations, explained in more detail below.

Regulations

Because Congress cannot legislate with the detail necessary to implement all its laws, the executive branch of government creates administrative agencies (such as the U.S. Department of Agriculture or the state Department of Motor Vehicles) to implement the law. Congress and state legislatures provide agencies the authority to promulgate rules and regulations to execute federal or state law. Federal regulations, as well as proposed regulations, are recorded in the Federal Register, a daily publication that reports the daily activities of the executive branch. When these regulations are made final, they are codified in the Code of Federal Regulations (CFR), a collection of all the regulations currently in force arranged by subject. Each state also has its own system for codifying its regulations. Federal regulations take effect nationally; state regulations can only be enforced within a particular state.

For example, in 1946, Congress passed the National School Lunch Program (NSLP), which reimburses schools for providing free and reduced lunch to their income-eligible students. To inform schools and the public about how the NSLP works, the U.S. Department of Agriculture (the agency created by the executive branch to make policy on farming, agriculture, and food) promulgated regulations that specified the program details. Here is an excerpt from the school lunch regulation:

If your client is concerned about their child's school lunch program, start by researching relevant state and federal regulations to support your argument that the lunch program does not meet minimum requirements.

(i) Requirements for lunch. School lunches offered to children aged five or older must meet, at a minimum, the meal requirements in paragraph (b) of this section. Schools must follow a food-based menu planning approach and produce enough food to offer each child the quantities specified in the meal pattern established in paragraph (c) of this section for each age/grade group served in the school. In addition, school lunches must meet the dietary specifications in paragraph (f) of this section. 7 C.F.R § 210.10 (2022).

Legislation Proposals

The executive branch proposes many of the bills that Congress considers. Similarly, a state's executive branch proposes bills that state legislators consider.

Executive Orders

Article II of the U.S. Constitution grants the President certain broad powers, including the power to issue executive orders. These orders, also called presidential directives, are effectively laws, but they do not need to be approved by Congress. Executive orders can be challenged in court, and legal scholars argue about the extent of presidential power to issue orders. The orders are numbered and recorded in the Federal Register and the CFR. Similarly, governors have the power to make executive orders. These orders do not require legislative approval, but they are binding.

THE JUDICIAL BRANCH

Overview

The federal judicial branch includes the U.S. Supreme Court and lower federal courts. Every state has its own judicial branch, including a state supreme court and inferior courts. Each system is responsible for deciding cases within its jurisdiction; the federal judiciary decides cases within the federal system, and each state system decides cases within its state.

Each state within the United States is its own jurisdiction under the law. One way to think of jurisdiction is in terms of geographic boundaries; the judicial branch in a state decides the outcome of criminal and civil cases within that geographic boundary. Moreover, the state and federal court systems operate in parallel. The federal system is not superior to the state system; while procedural rules allow the systems to interact, each state is its own jurisdiction, independent of the federal system.

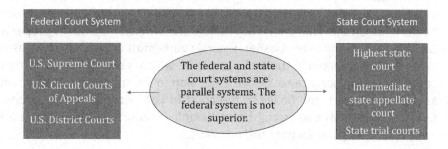

Courts make law. They decide disputes between individuals, and their decisions in those suits are binding on those individuals. In some cases, those decisions become precedent, which means that judges deciding a later case, within the same jurisdiction, must use that previous decision, or precedent, from a higher court to guide their decision in the case before them. Remember that a case usually begins in the lowest court (the trial court) and typically goes no further because it is either resolved or settled. Some cases are appealed to higher courts, and it is in these decisions, which are recorded and published, where the courts make law. As mentioned before, the appellate cases you read all started with a client who had a problem. This case law makes up a large portion of the law that lawyers must use to help solve their clients' problems. Statutes make up the other portion of the law.

Legal cases fall into two main categories: civil and criminal. Civil cases are lawsuits to recover damages or to stop others from doing something. These are normally disputes among private individuals and businesses, though government institutions can also be party to civil actions. Conversely, criminal cases are lawsuits that seek punishment in the form of imprisonment or fine. In criminal cases, the government brings a lawsuit on behalf of the public against an individual who violated a criminal law. In a civil suit, the party bringing the lawsuit is the plaintiff, and the party defending the lawsuit is the defendant. In a criminal suit, the accused is called the defendant, and the party bringing the case is called the State, the Government, the People, or the Commonwealth.

The Federal Court System

The federal courts are only permitted to hear limited types of cases; they are courts of limited jurisdiction. The Constitution specifies the types of cases the U.S. Supreme Court can hear. When Congress created the federal trial courts and intermediate courts, it passed laws defining what types of cases the lower federal courts could hear.

Generally, the federal courts hear cases that involve questions of federal law, including the U.S. Constitution, federal statutes, cases in which the United States is a party, and cases involving U.S. citizens and citizens of other countries. They also hear state law cases between citizens of different states; however, when the issue is an area where state law governs, such as property law that involves no federal issues, federal courts must apply state law. Cases in federal courts begin at the trial court level, which is called the U.S. district court. The losing party can appeal the decision to the appellate court, known as the circuit court, and finally to the court of last resort, the U.S. Supreme Court. Congress has also established other inferior courts in the federal court system, including bankruptcy and tax courts.

U.S. District Courts

The U.S. District Court is the lowest level of federal courts, also known as the trial court. This is where a litigant's case will usually enter the court system. This is the only level in the lawsuit where parties have the chance to present evidence to support their claims. Judges usually determine issues of law, and the jury examines the evidence of the parties (facts) and how those facts apply to the law. In a bench trial or a trial without a jury, a judge will decide the facts and apply the law to the facts. Every state has at least one U.S. District Court; some have more than one.

The kinds of cases heard in a U.S. District Court include criminal cases involving violation of federal laws (e.g., kidnapping, bank robbery, or drug trafficking), civil cases involving claims that a federal law has been violated (e.g., the Constitution or U.S. treaties), civil cases between parties of different states alleging violation of state law for amounts in excess of $75,000 (these are cases brought under "diversity jurisdiction"), and civil actions brought by or against the United States. The U.S. district court also hears appeals of certain federal agency decisions, such as Social Security Appeals Council decisions.

U.S. Circuit Courts of Appeals

The United States has 13 circuit courts. The federal circuit courts are appellate courts. The nation is divided geographically into 11 circuit boundaries, each with a circuit court. The two additional circuits include the Federal Circuit Court that sits in Washington, D.C., and the Federal Circuit, a federal appeals court of limited jurisdiction. A party dissatisfied with a district court ruling can appeal to the circuit court within his or her jurisdiction, except in criminal cases where the court finds the accused not guilty. There is no appeal of a not guilty verdict, and the case ends with the verdict. Generally, the circuit courts do not review the facts of the cases that have come before them. They accept the facts that have been found by either a jury or a judge. The circuit courts examine whether mistakes exist in the lower court's decision about what the law is and how it applies to the facts of a given case. Hence, no additional evidence is taken at this stage. Occasionally, a circuit court will review facts, but only if there has been a clearly erroneous decision regarding the facts. A circuit court normally sits in panels of three when hearing appeals. The diagram below depicts the federal circuit courts.

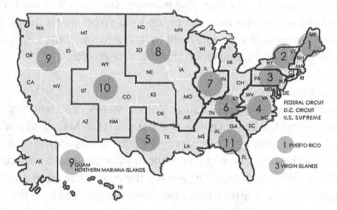

https://www.counselpress.com/images/map/us_circuit_rollover.gif.

U.S. Supreme Court

The Supreme Court is the highest court of the land and is in Washington, D.C. The Supreme Court is also an appellate court. Parties dissatisfied with a circuit court decision or a state supreme court decision (if it involves federal law — more on that later) can petition the U.S. Supreme Court through a "petition for a writ of certiorari" to hear their case. Not all cases get to the Supreme Court. The Court decides to hear a case when four justices agree to hear it. The Court is made up of nine justices, and all the justices sit in all cases before the Court. Most cases are never heard by the U.S. Supreme Court. Approximately 10,000 cases are submitted to the Court annually, and only about 75 to 80 are accepted.

The State Court System

Like the federal system, most state courts have three levels of courts: a trial court where most lawsuits begin, an intermediate court, and the highest court. However, some states, including New Hampshire, Nevada, Montana, and Vermont, among others, have only two levels: a trial court and a supreme court.

Trial Courts

Almost all state courts have two kinds of trial courts: a court of limited jurisdiction that hears special cases (probate, family, juvenile, municipal, traffic matters, etc.) and a court that hears criminal and civil matters.

Intermediate Courts

Many, but not all, states have appellate courts between their trial courts and their highest court. Intermediate courts are normally based on districts or counties. Dissatisfied parties to a lawsuit in a trial court may appeal to an appropriate intermediate court. The intermediate courts of appeal generally deal with mistakes in the law and procedural errors made in the trial court. Occasionally, intermediate courts will review a lower court's findings of fact, but typically this occurs only when there is a clear error.

Highest State Court

Every state has a highest court. Not all states call their highest courts "supreme courts." For instance, the highest courts in Maryland and New York are their courts of appeals. Confusingly, New York calls its trial courts supreme courts. The highest courts of states without intermediate courts directly hear appeals from their trial courts. Otherwise, the highest court in a state chooses which cases it will hear after a party petitions the court to hear the case, much like the U.S. Supreme Court. The highest state courts may have original jurisdiction in certain controversies. The highest court in a state is the highest authority on all state law issues within that jurisdiction. In matters involving federal law, however, a party may attempt to appeal to the U.S. Supreme Court.

 Video Quiz

One last point. The State of Magnolia. In Chapter 5 you will meet your client, Cleo Clover. Cleo Clover's case arose within the fictional jurisdiction, Magnolia. Magnolia is the equivalent of a state in the United States, e.g., New Hampshire or New York. Your client, Cleo Clover, has been charged with Driving Under the Influence (DUI) in Magnolia. The DUI statute passed by the Magnolia legislature and court opinions from the Magnolia Supreme Court will govern the outcome of your client's situation. As discussed in Chapter 4, the laws promulgated by the various branches of government within a state control the outcomes of legal cases brought before the courts within that jurisdiction. The case will be brought in a trial court in Magnolia because all legal disputes that go to litigation begin in a trial court within the governing jurisdiction.

How We Use the Law: Hierarchy of Law

INTRODUCTION

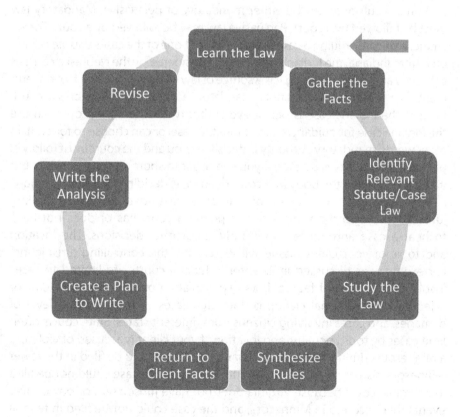

In this chapter, we are still learning the law. Lawyers look for legal solutions to their clients' problems. The law or rules they look for depend on the facts of each client's case. Once a lawyer identifies the legal issue or issues that the client's problem fits into (e.g., age discrimination in employment; admission of a prior bad act in a criminal trial), the next step is to look for the law that answers the problem.

HIERARCHY OF LAW

There is a hierarchy of law: primary authority and secondary authority. You will rely on primary authority (the actual rules of law) when you answer your client's problem. Specifically, primary authority includes constitutions, statutes, regulations, and judicial opinions. You cannot rely on secondary authority (e.g., journal articles, legal dictionaries) because secondary sources are not law; instead, secondary authority can help you learn more about a legal topic, locate more law on a topic, or bolster your legal argument (e.g., through law journals or legal encyclopedias). The law you rely on to answer your client's problem will depend on several factors, such as what state you are in and whether the legal issue is addressed by federal or state law.

Primary authority can be either mandatory or persuasive. Mandatory law must be followed by a court. Persuasive law may be followed by a court. For example, if you are arguing a case in Nebraska, but one of the cases you are relying on is from Indiana, the Indiana case will be considered by the Nebraska court as a primary authority (meaning it is a source of law created by a branch of government), but the Indiana case is not a mandatory authority on the Nebraska court. Instead, the Indiana case is persuasive authority; the Nebraska court can use the Indiana case for guidance, can ignore the case, or can choose to follow it. In other words, mandatory authority is decisive—you and the court must follow it; persuasive authority is guiding—you can use it to shore up your position, but it is not binding on the body (the court or agency) deciding the legal question.

To determine the weight of authority, first identify the controlling jurisdiction. Jurisdiction refers to the power a court has or does not have to hear a case and, more importantly, enforce its decisions. The location and topic of your client's issue will determine the controlling jurisdiction. For example, as discussed in Chapter 3, federal courts are limited to cases involving violations of federal laws (e.g., violation of federal criminal law or a federal constitutional claim), certain civil cases with a specified level of damages, and cases involving citizens from different states. State courts often limit cases by topic, penalty, and location. If your client is accused of violating a Minnesota criminal law, such as assault, the case would be filed in the lower Minnesota district court that hears criminal cases. The case could not be filed in a Virginia court because Virginia does not have jurisdiction or power over events that occurred in Minnesota, and the case could not be filed in federal court because a federal court does not have jurisdiction or power over cases involving state criminal law violations. Without a violation of federal law or a scenario described above, the federal court does not have jurisdiction to hear the case. Once you identify the court and controlling jurisdiction, you can determine the mandatory authority for that court.

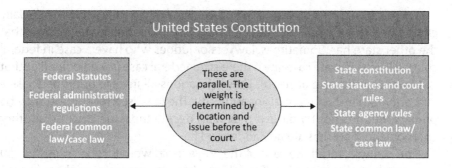

Mandatory authority is vertical. In the federal system, a decision by a circuit court is only binding on lower courts within that circuit. For example, a decision by the First Circuit Court of Appeals is only binding in the U.S. District Courts of Maine, New Hampshire, Massachusetts, Puerto Rico, and Rhode Island. The opinions of one circuit court are persuasive authority to another circuit court and U.S. district courts under other circuits.

The federal and state systems are parallel. One system does not trump the other system. Instead, both have a vertical hierarchy within their own systems.

Decisions by state trial courts and U.S. district courts carry the least weight. A decision by a particular trial court or U.S. District Court in a jurisdiction is not binding on other trial courts in that jurisdiction. However, lower court opinions can be persuasive to other lower courts or even higher courts within the same jurisdiction. This is especially true when a trial court has written an opinion that is precisely on point with an issue before another court. Your citation quickly identifies the level of the court in that jurisdiction and, thus, the weight of its authority.

When you are new to a state, it is helpful to look up a picture of the court system so you can visualize the hierarchy of the court system. For example, relevant to your client who is accused of violating a Minnesota criminal statute, this is a visualization of the Minnesota court structure:

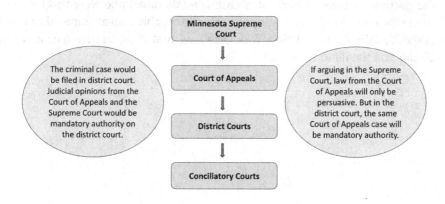

Quite often, lawyers and judges turn to another state's law—especially case law—if their own state has not addressed a particular legal issue that the other state has. Sometimes, lawyers or judges who have a case in federal court will look to state case law if there is no federal case law on point (i.e., that is relevant to the case at hand). These situations all involve using persuasive authority rather than mandatory authority. The law used for support may be primary, but it is not binding. It may help decide the issue because another court or legal body has already addressed it.

For example, recall the case of the 60-year-old woman who comes to you because she believes she was fired due to her age, not because she is incompetent. Let's say that the state you are in has a state statute that prohibits discrimination based on age. That statute is the primary authority that is also mandatory. Now, imagine that you are gathering research, and you find cases from your state's highest court that interpret the statute's language. Those cases are also mandatory authority. In addition, you realize that another state has a very similar antidiscrimination statute and some cases that interpret that state's statute. Because the cases interpret a statute very similar to your state statute, the cases have persuasive value. In other words, you can use the cases to shore up and support your position, but these cases have persuasive weight, not mandatory, binding weight on the court that will hear the client's case.

The case below (*Diaz v. Krob*) is an example where the parties and the court used other states' laws to help decide an issue that had not yet been addressed in their own state. In this case, a woman was crossing a street when she stopped at the center median because the "Don't Walk" warning activated. A school bus driver stopped and motioned her to cross in front of the bus, and the woman was struck and injured by a car. One issue in the case was whether the school bus driver had a duty to the woman whom he signaled (you will recognize the concept of "duty" from your torts class). Notice in the paragraph beginning with a "6," the court says, "The parties assert that the issue of whether a duty exists under the circumstances of this case is one of first impression in Illinois. The parties cite various out-of-state rulings in support of their respective positions." Because there are no similar cases in Illinois, the parties are using other states' case law (Michigan and New York) to persuade the court in Illinois to adopt their position. This is an example of primary authority (Michigan and New York case law) that is persuasive (i.e., it is not binding on the Illinois court).

264 Ill.App.3d 97
Appellate Court of Illinois,
Third District.

Janet L. DIAZ and Jaime Diaz, wife and
husband, Plaintiffs-Appellants,
v.
Grace KROB and Joliet Township High School District
#204, Defendants-Appellees.
No. 3-93-0852. | June 30, 1994.

Pedestrian whom automobile struck after school bus driver motioned for pedestrian to cross street sued school district for negligence. The Circuit Court, 12th Judicial Circuit, Will County, Herman S. Haase, J., dismissed complaint. Pedestrian appealed. The Appellate Court, Breslin, J., held that defendants did not owe pedestrian duty.

Affirmed.

West Headnotes [Omitted. . . .]

Opinion

Justice BRESLIN delivered the opinion of the court:

The plaintiffs, Janet L. Diaz and Jaime Diaz, filed this lawsuit against the defendants, Grace Krob (school bus driver) and Joliet Township High School District #204, for damages and loss of consortium from injuries Janet allegedly sustained when she was struck by an automobile after the school bus driver motioned for her to cross a street. The trial court dismissed the complaint finding that the defendants did not owe the plaintiffs a duty as a matter of law. We affirm.

The accident happened when Janet attempted to cross Collins Street, in Joliet, Illinois. The complaint alleged that as she proceeded west within the crosswalk, the "Don't Walk" warning sign activated. Thus, she stopped at the median dividing traffic on the street. At that point, the school bus driver, who was stopped immediately to the north of the crosswalk at the red light, motioned or waved to the plaintiff to continue walking across the street in front of the bus.

The complaint further alleged that the bus driver knew or should have known that the bus prevented the plaintiff from seeing traffic proceeding south on Collins Street in the lane nearest the curb. The

complaint also alleged that as a proximate result of the bus driver's negligence in gesturing to the plaintiff to continue walking across the street the plaintiff suffered an injury when she was struck by a vehicle.

In response to these allegations, the defendants filed a motion to dismiss pursuant to section 2-615 of the Civil Practice Law (735 ILCS 5/2-615 (West 1992)) alleging that the plaintiffs failed to allege sufficient facts to give rise to a duty. The trial court agreed with the defendants and dismissed the complaint.

*99 A motion to dismiss under section 2-615 admits all well-pleaded facts in the complaint for purposes of the motion. (Sisk v. Williamson County (1994), 261 Ill.App.3d 49, 198 Ill.Dec. 342, 632 N.E.2d 672.) A cause of action will not be dismissed on the pleadings unless it clearly appears that no set of facts can be proved which will entitle the plaintiff to recover. (Charles Hester Enterprises, Inc. v. Illinois Founders Insurance Co. (1986), 114 Ill.2d 278, 102 Ill. Dec. 306, 499 N.E.2d 1319.)

[The starred numbers track the page numbers of the case as if it appeared in the print book version of the reporter. You will need these page numbers for the pin cite in your citation.]

One of the necessary elements of a negligence cause of action is the existence of a duty which requires a person to conform to a certain standard of conduct for the purpose of protecting the plaintiff from an unreasonable risk of harm. (Swett v. Village of Algonquin (1988), 169 Ill. App. 3d 78, 119 Ill.Dec. 838, 523 N.E.2d 594; Mitchell v. City of Chicago (1991), 221 Ill. App.3d 1017, 164 Ill.Dec. 506, 583 N.E.2d 60.) It is not sufficient that the plaintiff's complaint merely alleges that a duty exists; the plaintiff must state facts from which the law will raise a duty. (Swett, 169 Ill.App.3d 78, 119 Ill.Dec. 838, 523 N.E.2d 594.) Factors relevant in determining whether a duty exists include the foreseeability of injury, the likelihood of injury, the magnitude of the burden of guarding against the injury, the consequence of placing that burden on the defendant, and the possible seriousness of the injury. (Deibert v. Bauer Brothers Construction Co. (1990), 141 Ill.2d 430, 152 Ill.Dec. 552, 566 N.E. 2d 239.) Whether a duty exists is a question of law to be determined by the court. (Mitchell, 221 Ill. App.3d 1017, 164 Ill.Dec. 506, 583 N.E.2d 60.)

Here, the court notes the parties' use of out-of-state case law to support their positions.

The parties assert that the issue of whether a duty exists under the circumstances of this case is one of first impression in Illinois. The parties cite various out-of-state rulings in support of their respective positions. (See Sweet v. Ringwelski (1961), 362 Mich. 138, 106 N.W.2d 742; Peka v. Boose (1988), 172 Mich.App. 139, 431 N.W.2d 399; Valdez v. Bernard (1986), 123 A.D.2d 351, 506 N.Y.S. 2d 363.)

In *Sweet*, the Michigan Supreme Court held that the trial court should not have granted a directed verdict in favor of the defendant truck driver on the ground of no showing of negligence. The defendant truck driver had stopped his truck and waved for the ten-year-old plaintiff pedestrian to cross the street on the crosswalk in front of him. The plaintiff continued crossing the street into the lane next to the truck and was struck by a car. The court's decision was based on the fact that the plaintiff was only ten years old, that her vision may have been obscured by the defendant's truck, and that she relied on what she considered to be directions from an adult.

In *Peka*, the defendant motioned for a southbound motorist to make a left turn. The southbound motorist followed the defendant's signal and struck the plaintiff's vehicle. The Michigan Appellate Court found that the signaling motorist owed no duty to the plaintiff. *100 The court found that Sweet was easily distinguishable on the basis that it involved a ten-year-old child who relied on the directions of an adult. The court found that the *Sweet* case should be limited to its facts.

In *Valdez*, the plaintiff was injured when she crossed a street after a bus driver had motioned for her to do so. The New York court noted that, under certain circumstances, a driver of a motor vehicle may be liable to a pedestrian where that driver undertakes to direct a pedestrian safely across the road in front of his vehicle and negligently carries out that duty. The court found, however, that the bus driver was not the proximate cause of the plaintiff's injury where the plaintiff interpreted the bus driver's wave to mean only that he would not move the bus while the plaintiff passed in front of it.

Applying the above-mentioned principles and case law, we hold that the trial court correctly found as a matter of law that the defendants did not owe the plaintiffs a duty under the facts of this case. Unlike the cases cited by the parties, the crosswalk at the intersection in question was controlled by a "Don't Walk" signal. Nonetheless, the instant plaintiff chose to ignore it and proceed across the remainder of the intersection. Unlike *Sweet*, the plaintiff was not a youngster who relied on the directions of an adult. While we agree that *Sweet* is good law, we do not go as far as *Valdez*, where it is implied that a duty would exist if the plaintiff interpreted the bus driver's gesture as something more than an indication that the driver would not move the bus until the plaintiff passed.

In this paragraph, the court provides its holding and how it relied on the out-of-state case law. Remember the Michigan and New York cases were only persuasive authority on this Illinois court.

We agree that an injury is foreseeable here. But whether a legal duty exists involves more than just foreseeability of possible harm; it also involves legal and social policies. (Swett, 169 Ill.App.3d 78, 119 Ill. Dec. 838, 523 N.E.2d 594.) Here, the magnitude of guarding against the injury and the consequence of placing that burden on the defendant weigh heavily in favor of finding no duty. An adult pedestrian with no obvious impairments should be held responsible for deciding whether gestures and directions given by a motorist can be safely followed. We simply do not believe that the instant bus driver's act of common courtesy should be transformed into a tort thereby giving the plaintiff license to proceed across an intersection against a warning light and without taking any precautions of her own.

For the forgoing reasons, the judgment of the circuit court of Will County is affirmed.

Affirmed.

 **Video Quiz**

PRACTICAL TIP

When identifying the best legal arguments, first use mandatory authority. Persuasive authority is helpful to bolster or shore up your argument, and it is essential when you have a legal issue of first impression in the jurisdiction where your case will be argued.

Mandatory Authority	Persuasive Authority
Must be followed by the court. Examples: • United States Constitution • United States Supreme Court • State appellate court ruling on lower courts in that state • Federal circuit court ruling on the courts within that circuit (First Circuit Court of Appeals rulings are binding on federal trial courts, U.S. district courts, in NH, ME, MA, RI, and PR—the jurisdictions that make up the First Circuit) • Federal statutes • State statutes within that state • Regulations • Agency rules	**May** be followed by the court. Examples: • State appellate court rulings in another state (e.g., a New Hampshire Supreme Court case may be persuasive to the Vermont Supreme Court in deciding a case but will not be mandatory authority) • Federal circuit court cases in another circuit • Lower trial court decisions within a state • Secondary sources (e.g., journal articles, legal dictionaries)

CHAPTER 5

Sample Case File

INTRODUCTION

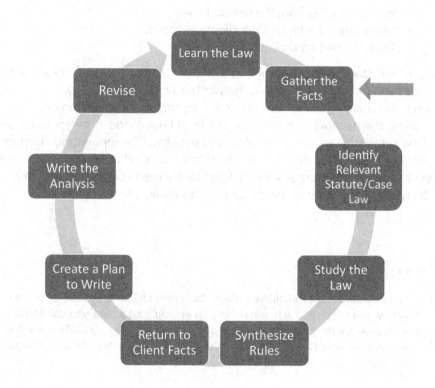

This chapter introduces our sample case file. Everything a lawyer does typically begins with a client and the client's legal problem. When you research and read a statute or a case, you should have your client's issue or legal question in mind to help guide you. Often your supervising attorney will send you a brief memorandum describing your client's facts along with instructions on what she wants you to do. Remember, solving your client's problem is a recursive process, not a linear process. Generally, these are the steps you will go through:

- Become familiar with the area of law.
- Gather facts of the client's case.
- Identify the client's issue or legal question from those facts.
- Identify relevant law that is likely to hold the answer to the legal question (e.g., employment law, medical malpractice law, criminal law).
- Create and execute a research plan.
- Read and study relevant statutes and cases, including identifying key facts in the case law.
- Synthesize rules from the relevant law.
- Identify decisive facts in the client's scenario.
- Begin the writing process.

At this stage, you are gathering the client's facts. Here, you are using the supervising attorney's memo to gather the facts. In practice, you may also interview a client and/or review police reports or other documents. Interviewing clients requires more than just legal knowledge. A lawyer must also show compassion, cultural humility, and patience. The supervising attorney's memo will help you identify the client's issue or legal question. Always read your supervising attorney's instructions carefully so you are not researching the wrong issue and wasting the client's money and/or your time.

PRACTICAL TIP

Lawyers refer to "issues" in different ways. Your client's legal issue is the legal question that you are tasked with answering. When you read a case, you will identify the *issue* before the court, or the legal question before the court. When reading the case, you should keep your client's *issue* in mind to extract relevant information to answer your client's legal question.

MEMORANDUM

To: Law Intern
From: Supervising Attorney
Date: XXX
Re: ***State v. Clover*—Driving Under the Influence**

As you know, Cleo Clover is our client, and we have represented him in a number of matters. Recently, he was stopped and arrested for Driving Under the Influence in Magnolia. There is no question that the breathalyzer is correct, that Mr. Clover is an adult, and that Mr. Clover was intoxicated when he was found asleep in his car. The only issue that you should address at this point is whether Mr. Clover was "driving." Mr. Clover was asleep in his car when the police arrived. The facts are included below.

From prior cases, I know that the statute and cases I have attached here are the key cases and statute on this issue in Magnolia as Mr. Clover was arrested in Sweetwater, Magnolia.

Cleo Clover wants to know whether he can be convicted of Driving Under the Influence (DUI). Mr. Clover provided the following facts in an interview with our firm.

On Friday, October XX, 20XX, Mr. Clover had been at an office party where he had been drinking. After midnight, he asked his co-worker, Robin Branch, to drive his car to her apartment building where he could leave his car and catch an Uber or walk the rest of the way home. Mr. Clover had not realized that he could not leave his car overnight at the apartment complex since he did not live there. The automatic gate arm to enter the paved parking lot was raised and stuck in the "up" position. It had been like that for the past year. Ms. Branch pulled into the parking lot and parked Mr. Clover's car in a space. At the entrance to the parking lot, there was a sign that said, "Resident parking only—All others will be towed."

Ms. Branch gave Mr. Clover back his key fob. He put it in his pocket and got back into the car to call an Uber. He, however, fell asleep, awakening only when a police officer knocked on his window. When the officer arrived, the engine was not on, but the heat and lights were running. Mr. Clover described his car as a 2021 Toyota Highlander, which permits access to accessories with a push of the ignition button. To ignite the engine, the key fob must be nearby, and the ignition button and brake are pressed at the same time. Instead, by pressing only the ignition button (without the brake), the accessories, such as lights and heat, can be used.

From the police report, I gathered that Officer Lena Starling observed a man, now known as Mr. Clover, asleep with his head back in the driver's seat of a parked car. Officer Starling noted that the engine was off, but the lights were on. Officer Starling knocked on the car window and stated that when Mr. Clover put the window down, she smelled alcohol and observed a dazed Mr. Clover with blood-shot eyes. Officer Starling asked Mr. Clover to exit the car and perform three field sobriety tests. The Officer identified Mr. Clover by his license and registration. He admitted he was impaired at the office party and asked his co-worker to drive him to her apartment. Mr. Clover said he fell asleep after giving up on summoning an Uber. He also admitted that he worried his car would be towed, so he stayed in the car to "sleep it off." Mr. Clover figured he could move the car if the parking space owner returned. Officer Starling stated that Mr. Clover failed his field sobriety tests and that his blood alcohol content was 0.11. During the arrest, Mr. Clover produced the key fob from his pocket.

In the first paragraph, the supervising attorney is identifying the area of law: here, criminal law, specifically, Driving Under the Influence.

When the supervisor states, "the only issue that you should address . . . ," this language tells us to limit our research to the one issue. Our specific legal question that we must research is whether Mr. Clover "drove."

Supervising attorney relates that the jurisdiction is the state of Magnolia because Mr. Clover is charged with DUI, a state crime, in Sweetwater, a city in Magnolia. The statute and cases appear later in this chapter.

Magnolia DUI Statute

Revised Statute Annotated of the State of Magnolia

Title XXI. Motor Vehicles

Chapter 265-A Alcohol or Drug Impairment (Refs & Annos)

Driving or Operating Under the Influence of Drugs or Liquor

265-A:2 Driving or Operating Under the Influence of Drugs or Liquor; Driving or Operating With Excess Alcohol Concentration

(I) No person shall drive or attempt to drive a vehicle upon the ways of this state open to the public or operate or attempt to operate an OHRV:

(a) While such person is under the influence of intoxicating liquor or any controlled drug or any combination of intoxicating liquor and controlled drugs; or

(b) While such person has an alcohol concentration of 0.08 or more, or in the case of a person under the age of 21, 0.02 or more.

(II) No person shall operate or attempt to operate a boat while under the influence of intoxicating liquor or a controlled drug or any combination of intoxicating liquor and a controlled drug or drugs, or while such person has an alcohol concentration of 0.08 or more, or in the case of persons under the age of 21, 0.02 or more.

Updated with laws currently effective May 6, 2020 through Chapter 8 of the 2020 Reg. Sess., not including changes and corrections made by the State of Magnolia, Office of Legislative Services.

State v. Holloran, 140 M.G. 563
669 A.2d 800

140 M.G. 563
Supreme Court of Magnolia.

The STATE of Magnolia
v.
Patrick W. HOLLORAN.
No. 94–558. |
Dec. 27, 1995.

Defendant was convicted before the Derry District Court, Warhall, J., of driving under the influence, and he appealed. The Supreme Court held that evidence was sufficient to find that defendant was in actual physical control of his truck, as required by conviction, notwithstanding that truck was legally parked, its lights were off, and engine was not running.

PER CURIAM.

After a bench trial, the Derry District Court (*Warhall,* J.) convicted the defendant, Patrick W. Holloran, of driving under the influence. *See* RSA 265-A:2 (Supp. 1994). On appeal, the defendant asserts that the trial court erred in denying his motion for a directed verdict based upon insufficiency of the evidence. We affirm.

801 In the evening of March 15, 1994, Londonderry Police Officer Mark Cagnetta approached a Chevrolet pickup truck with its lights off parked on Symmes Drive in Londonderry. The officer saw the defendant sitting alone behind the wheel. Cagnetta "spotlighted" the truck and the defendant quickly jumped out. Cagnetta told the defendant to get back into the truck, observing that the defendant appeared "unsteady" on his feet.

The defendant explained that he was waiting for a call from his wife to pick her up from a Tupperware party in Auburn. The officer did not see a phone, and the defendant indicated that he had a pager. Cagnetta noticed that the defendant's breath smelled of an alcoholic beverage, that his eyes were glassy and bloodshot, and that he appeared disheveled.

The officer also observed that although the engine was not running, the keys to the truck were in the ignition. The defendant stated that he had been at the airport and had come to Symmes Drive to wait for his wife, but that he had had nothing to drink that evening and should have remained at the airport. After the defendant failed three field sobriety tests, Cagnetta arrested him for driving while under the influence of alcohol.

At the close of the State's case, the defendant moved for a directed verdict, arguing that the evidence was insufficient for a rational trier of fact to find, beyond a reasonable doubt, that he had driven his truck on the night of the arrest. The court denied the motion and found the defendant guilty, sentencing him to a fine, ninety-day license revocation, and mandatory attendance in an alcohol awareness program. This appeal followed.

The defendant was convicted of violating RSA 265-A:2. "The *actus reus* contemplated in RSA 265-A:2 is 'driv[ing]' a motor vehicle while under the influence of alcohol." *State v. Willard,* 139 M.G. 568, 570, 660 A.2d 1086, 1087 (1995). "Driv[ing]" has been defined as "operat[ing]" or being in "actual physical control" of a motor vehicle. RSA 259:24 (1993). Because the State does not allege that the defendant was operating his truck, the question before us is whether *565 a rational trier of fact, viewing the evidence most favorably to the State, could have found beyond a reasonable doubt that the defendant was in actual physical control of the truck.

"To have 'actual physical control' of a motor vehicle, one must have the capacity bodily to guide or exercise dominion over the vehicle at the present time." *Willard,* 139 M.G. at 571, 660 A.2d at 1088 (emphasis omitted). What constitutes "actual physical control" will vary depending upon the facts of the case, but "the primary focus of the inquiry is whether the person is merely using the vehicle as a stationary shelter or whether it is reasonable to assume that the person will, while under the influence, jeopardize the public by exercising some measure of control over the vehicle." *Atkinson v. State,* 331 M.G. 199, 627 A.2d 1019, 1028 (1993).

Specifically, in *Atkinson,* the defendant was not in actual physical control of his vehicle when he was asleep in the driver's seat with keys in the ignition, engine off, in a legally parked motor vehicle because there was no circumstantial or other evidence that the defendant climbed into his vehicle, put the key in the ignition, and went to sleep. *Id*. at 1029. In interpreting the statute to avoid a "Parked While Intoxicated" crime, we stated:

> The legislature has the desire to prevent intoxicated individuals from posing a serious public risk with their vehicles. However, we do not believe the legislature meant to forbid those intoxicated individuals who emerge from a tavern at closing time on a cold winter night from merely entering their vehicles to seek shelter while they sleep off the effects of alcohol. As long as such individuals do not act to endanger themselves or others, they do not present the hazard to which the drunk driving statute is directed. While we wish to discourage intoxicated individuals from first testing their drunk driving skills before deciding to pull over, this should not prevent us from allowing people too drunk to drive, and prudent enough not to try to seek shelter in their legally parked cars.

Id. at 1025-26.

At trial, the State adduced only circumstantial evidence to prove that the defendant had "actual physical control" of his truck. "[C]ircumstantial evidence which excludes any other rational conclusion is sufficient to establish beyond a reasonable doubt the *actus reus* set out in a motor vehicle statute." *Willard*, 139 M.G. at 571, 660 A.2d at 1088 (quotation and ellipses omitted). In applying this standard "we examine each evidentiary item in the context of all the evidence, not in isolation." *State v. Bissonnette*, 138 M.G. 82, 85, 635 A.2d 468, 469 (1993).

The defendant argues that because the truck was legally parked, the lights were off, and the engine was not running, it is speculative to conclude that he would soon be operating the vehicle. These acts alone, however, are not dispositive. When Officer Cagnetta came upon the truck, the defendant was in the driver's seat. The defendant **802 exhibited signs of drunkenness, and he told the officer that he was waiting for a call to pick up his wife, who was in another town. The keys were in the ignition. In the context of the officer's observations and the defendant's statements, a rational trier of fact could find beyond a reasonable doubt that the defendant was not merely Parked While Intoxicated but would be imminently operating the truck in an inebriated condition, and, therefore, that he was in actual physical control of the vehicle. *See Willard*, 139 M.G. at 571, 660 A.2d at 1088.

Affirmed.

BRODERICK, J., did not sit; the others concurred.

All Citations

140 M.G. 563, 669 A.2d 800

State v. Winstead, 150 M.G. 244 (2003)
836 A.2d 775

Supreme Court of Magnolia

The STATE of Magnolia

v.

William T. Winstead

No. 2002-660

Argued October 9, 2003
Opinion Issued November 12, 2003

Synopsis

Following a bench trial, defendant was convicted in the District Court, Claremont County, Yazinski, J., of driving under the influence (DUI).

Defendant appealed. The Supreme Court, Duggan, J., held that sufficient evidence existed that defendant was in actual physical control of car before he fell asleep to support conviction.

Affirmed.

Attorneys and Law Firms

**776 *245 Peter W. Heed, attorney general (Jonathan V. Gallo, assistant attorney general, on the brief and orally), for the State.

Nancy S. Tierney, of Lebanon, by brief and orally, for the defendant.

Opinion

DUGGAN, J.

Following a bench trial in Claremont District Court (Yazinski, J.), the defendant, William T. Winstead, was found guilty of driving while intoxicated. *See* RSA 265-A:2 (Supp. 2002). On appeal, he contends that: (1) the trial court erred when it admitted the results of his blood alcohol test; (2) he was denied equal protection

of the law; and (3) the evidence was insufficient to prove he was in control of the vehicle. We affirm.

The record supports the following facts. The charge arose out of an incident on April 6, 2002, when, at approximately 3:13 a.m., Officer Shawn L. Hallock of the Claremont Police Department discovered the defendant in a car in the Wal-Mart parking lot. The defendant was sleeping upright in the driver's seat, with the car engine running. At trial, the defendant testified that he decided to sleep in his car because he was "not . . . capable to drive anywhere," and that the car was running so he could stay warm. The defendant further testified that while he had no intention of driving the car, he did unlock the door, sit in the driver's seat, push the clutch in, move the gear selector to neutral, start the engine, and turn on the heater.

Hallock approached the car and attempted to wake the defendant. When the defendant awoke and spoke with Hallock, Hallock "immediately smelled an odor of intoxicant." The defendant admitted to Hallock that he had consumed a six- pack of Bacardi Silvers that evening. Hallock asked the defendant to perform field sobriety tests, which the defendant failed. Hallock subsequently arrested the defendant for driving while intoxicated.

After his arrest, the defendant was taken to the Claremont Police Department where he read and signed the Administrative License Suspension form, which authorized the police to perform any combination of breath, blood, urine or physical testing. The defendant was first given an intoxilyzer breath test, which resulted in a blood alcohol content (BAC) of 0.07. The result of the defendant's intoxilyzer test was below the statutorily defined level (BAC of 0.08) for *prima facie* evidence of intoxication. *See* RSA 265-A:2. Hallock then asked the defendant to take a blood test. The defendant testified that Hallock requested a blood test only for drugs. The defendant's blood was tested for both drugs and alcohol, *246 which resulted in a BAC of 0.08. The results of both tests were admitted at trial without objection. The district court found the defendant guilty and denied his motion to reconsider. This appeal followed.

On appeal, the defendant first argues that the district court erred in admitting the blood test results. The defendant contends that the police were not entitled to conduct further testing after the intoxilyzer test revealed a BAC of 0.07 and that the defendant consented only to a blood test for drugs, not alcohol. We conclude, however, that the issue was not preserved for appellate review.

"The general rule in this jurisdiction is that a contemporaneous and specific objection **777 is required to preserve an issue for appellate review." *State v. Brinkman*, 136 M.G. 716, 718, 621 A.2d 932 (1993) (quotation omitted). In addition, "[t]he objection must state 'explicitly the specific ground of objection.' " *Id.* (quoting *M.G. R. Ev.* 103(b)(1)). "This requirement, grounded in common sense and judicial economy, affords the trial court an opportunity to correct an error it may have made...." *Brinkman*, 136 M.G. at 718, 621 A.2d 932.

At trial, the State questioned Officer Hallock about the blood test performed on the defendant. The State then offered the certified lab results of the blood test as Exhibit 4. The following colloquy ensued:

[STATE]: State would enter Exhibit 4.

[COURT]: Any objection, Ms. Tierney?

[DEFENSE]: No, Your Honor.

Because the defendant failed to make "a contemporaneous and specific objection" to the admission of the blood test results, *id.*, the issue was not preserved for appellate review.

The defendant next argues that his right to equal protection was violated because Officer Hallock testified that he does not typically disturb people parked in recreational vehicles (RVs) in the Wal- Mart parking lot. Thus, the defendant argues, he was treated differently because he was in a car. We conclude, however, that this issue was also not preserved for appellate review.

"This court has consistently held that we will not consider issues raised on appeal that were not presented in the lower court." *State v. McAdams*, 134 M.G. 445, 447, 594 A.2d 1273 (1991) (quotation omitted). Where the defendant raises a constitutional claim, it must be brought to the attention of the trial court in order to preserve the issue for appeal. *State v. Patterson*, 145 M.G. 462, 466-67, 764 A.2d 901 (2000).

*247 At trial, defense counsel made three references to the different treatment afforded the defendant's car as opposed to an RV. First, defense counsel questioned Officer Hallock on cross-examination about another RV present in the Wal-Mart parking lot on the night the defendant was arrested. Second, defense counsel questioned Officer Hallock about whether, in general, he would knock on the door of an RV that was running. Finally, as part of closing argument, the defense argued: "Officer Hallock indicated that if he had been in the RV, he would have never bothered. The mere fact he was in a Subaru, or a Saturn, is what caused his eyes to light up. The kind of vehicle you're in shouldn't be determinative." In addition, in a motion to reconsider, the defense stated that one "area[ ] of law to be reviewed" included "[w]ere there grounds for waking him if, according to testimony, he would not have been disturbed if he had been in an RV."

Aside from these general references to the different treatment afforded persons in cars and RVs, no constitutional argument was raised at the trial court. At no point during the trial or in the motion to reconsider did defense counsel assert that the defendant's right to equal protection was being violated. Because the defendant failed to "bring the constitutional claim to the attention of the trial court, the issue is not preserved for appeal, and we decline to review it." *Id.* at 467, 764 A.2d 901.

Finally, the defendant argues that because he was asleep, only turned on the heat and had no intent to drive the car, there was insufficient evidence for the trial court to find that he was in control of the car and thus operating a vehicle under the influence. We must determine "whether a rational trier of fact . . . could have found beyond a reasonable doubt that the defendant was in actual physical control of the **778 [vehicle]." *State v. Holloran*, 140 M.G. 563, 564-65, 669 A.2d 800 (1995) (per curiam); *see* RSA 265-A:2; RSA 259:24 (1993).

"To have 'actual physical control' of a motor vehicle, one must have the capacity bodily to guide or exercise dominion over the vehicle at the present time." *State v. Willard,* 139 M.G. 568, 571, 660 A.2d 1086 (1995) (emphasis omitted). Circumstantial evidence of imminent operation is also sufficient for actual physical control. *See id.* Accordingly, while a person who is sound asleep cannot have such a capacity, "circumstantial evidence which excludes any other rational conclusion is sufficient . . . to establish beyond a reasonable doubt the *actus reus* set out in a motor vehicle statute." *Id.* (quotation omitted).

This case is indistinguishable from *Willard.* In *Willard,* the defendant was found asleep in the driver's seat of his vehicle in a parking lot with the vehicle's engine idling. A police officer woke him, determined he was intoxicated and arrested him for driving while intoxicated. In holding that *248 a rational trier of fact could find that the defendant was in *actual physical control* of the vehicle, we noted that "if circumstantial evidence were to prove that [the] defendant [ ] started his car before falling asleep, he would have been in actual physical control of it while awake and in the driver's seat." *Id.;* see also *Atkinson v. State,* 331 M.G. 199, 627 A.2d 1019, 1028 (1993) ("Indeed, once an individual has started the vehicle, he or she has come as close as possible to actually [operating it] without doing so and will generally be in 'actual physical control' of the vehicle.").

Here, the defendant was also found asleep in the driver's seat of a car in a parking lot with the engine running. Moreover, the defendant testified at trial that he unlocked the door, sat in the driver's seat, pushed the clutch in, moved the gear selector to neutral, started the engine and turned on the heater. Given these facts and the reasonable inferences therefrom, a rational trier of fact could find beyond a reasonable doubt that the defendant was in actual physical control of the car before he fell asleep. *See Willard,* 139 M.G. at 571, 660 A.2d 1086.

Affirmed.

BROCK, C.J., and BRODERICK, NADEAU and DALIANIS, JJ., concurred.

All Citations

150 M.G. 244, 836 A.2d 775

END OF DOCUMENT

State v. O'Malley, 120 M.G. 507 (2002)
416 A.2d 1387

120 M.G. 507
Supreme Court of Magnolia.

The STATE of Magnolia
v.

John T. O'MALLEY.
No. 79-374.|
June 25, 2002.

Synopsis

Defendant was convicted before the Trial Court, Rockingham County, Randall, J., of operating a motor vehicle while under the influence of intoxicating liquor and of operating a motor vehicle after a license had been revoked, and he appealed. The Supreme Court, King, J., held that absent evidence establishing beyond a reasonable doubt that defendant operated the subject motor vehicle, which was parked on public way with the engine off and with defendant asleep behind the wheel, defendant's mere presence in the nonmoving vehicle was insufficient to establish that he was in actual physical control of the vehicle.

Reversed.

Attorneys and Law Firms

**1388 *508 Gregory H. Smith, Acting Atty. Gen. (Deborah J. Cooper, Asst. Atty. Gen. orally), for the State.

James A. Connor, Manchester, by brief and orally, for defendant.

Opinion

KING, Justice.

This is an appeal from a verdict by the Trial Court (Randall, J.) finding the defendant guilty of operating a motor vehicle while under the influence of intoxicating liquor, second offense, RSA 265-A:2, and of operating a motor vehicle after a license had been revoked. RSA 262:27-b.

On March 17, 2000, police officers observed a vehicle parked off Ladybug Lane, a public way, in front of Arthur Lambro's house. The officers testified that the keys were in the ignition, but the vehicle engine was off. The officers further testified that they observed the defendant in the driver's seat with his head slumped over and his eyes closed. After the officers knocked on the vehicle's window without a response from the defendant, they opened the door and observed several empty and full beer bottles and detected an odor of alcohol.

After being awakened by one of the officers, even though the engine was off, the defendant allegedly pushed in the clutch and tried to shift the gear. The defendant was then asked to step out of the car and produce his license and registration. Defendant responded that he had no license. The officer then assisted the defendant to the police vehicle as the defendant stumbled, staggered, and nearly fell. The officer performed field sobriety tests on the defendant. During the course of the balancing tests, defendant swayed 5-6 inches front to rear and almost fell. In the performance of the finger-to-nose test, the defendant twice missed his nose with both hands. The defendant was then placed under arrest for operating a motor vehicle while intoxicated, second offense, and for operating after revocation.

The primary issue on this appeal is whether the trial *509 court erred in ruling that the defendant was, in fact, in actual physical control of the vehicle. In the instant case, the uncontroverted evidence is that the defendant was asleep and even though the keys were in the ignition, the car was not on or moving. Circumstantial evidence which excludes any other rational conclusion is sufficient, however, to establish beyond a reasonable doubt that a person was exercising dominion over the automobile. State v. Costello, 110 M.G. 182, 263, A.2d 671 (1970); see State v. Martin, 116 M.G. 47, 351 A.2d 52 (1976).

Defendant testified that he had not operated nor intended to operate the motor vehicle, that he had hitchhiked to Arthur Lambro's house, and that at some time later that evening, Lambro suggested that the defendant "[g]o warm up the car and I'll get my coat and drive you home." He testified he went out to

Lambro's car and fell asleep. We find that the defendant's account of what transpired was not unreasonable and note that the State offered no evidence to dispute defendant's testimony.

The State must prove beyond a reasonable doubt that the defendant drove the motor vehicle upon a public way in this State while under the influence of intoxicating liquor. State v. Costello supra (dissenting opinion); see State v. Scanlon supra. We hold, as a matter of law, that in the absence of evidence which establishes beyond a reasonable doubt that the defendant drove or would imminently operate the motor vehicle, the defendant's mere presence in a nonmoving vehicle is insufficient to meet the State's burden.

Reversed.

All Citations

120 M.G. 507, 416 A.2d 1387

END OF DOCUMENT

CHAPTER 6

How to Read, Understand, and Brief Statutes and Cases

INTRODUCTION

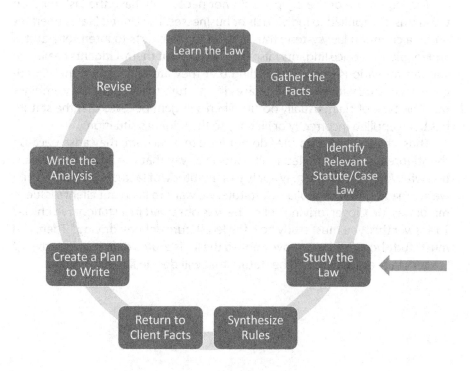

In this chapter, we show you how to study the law, specifically, how to read and interpret a statute and read case law so that you understand what the court is saying and doing. When a statute exists, the statute is the controlling law for the case. We will start with the statute, which is controlling law, in our sample case file.

READING AND UNDERSTANDING A STATUTE

You will learn how to locate criminal statutes. If using an online source such as Westlaw or Lexis, start with your controlling jurisdiction (e.g., the state where your client was arrested) and then type in the behavior that is regulated or prohibited. The left-hand tool bar allows you to limit your search to statutes, case law, and other content types.

In Mr. Clover's case, you have learned that Mr. Clover was charged in Magnolia with Driving Under the Influence. Once you have found the relevant statute, you must study it and identify what it prohibits.

Recall that statutes come from the legislative branch of government. What is contained in a statute is primary authority because a statute is law created from a branch of government. Statutory law (from the legislature) or regulatory law (from agencies) can govern criminal and civil conduct. Although the sample case file does not require you to examine a regulation, it is helpful to remember that in any given legal problem, your research may lead you to a statute, which in turn may lead you to a regulation. Agencies enact regulatory rules to carry out laws enacted by the legislature (either state or federal). Remember the woman who believes she was fired because of her age? The employer's conduct would be regulated by federal or state statutes or regulations that govern civil behavior.

The legislature or the agencies do not necessarily have the last word on the law as it is applied to individuals or businesses. The United States operates under a common law system; thus, it is up to the courts to interpret statutes and regulations once litigants raise questions about them. Litigants challenge statutes for various reasons, including that they are unconstitutional. Or litigants take issue with words or phrases in a statute that are arguably ambiguous. This type of claim usually occurs when a litigant believes that the statute has been applied incorrectly or illegally to the litigant's situation.

Thus, challenges to statutes do not arise in a vacuum; they arise because the statute has been applied to litigants in a way that the litigants believe is unlawful. A particular law may apply to a multitude of factual situations. When we are reading the Magnolia DUI statute, we want to keep our client's issue in mind: was Mr. Clover "driving" when he was observed in a stationary vehicle? To answer this, you must study how the legislature defines "driving." Then, you must study how the courts have applied the legislature's definition of "driving."

Let's take a close look at the statute that will decide Mr. Clover's fate:

Magnolia DUI Statute

This is the name the Magnolia legislature has given the state statute.

Revised Statute Annotated of the State of Magnolia

Title XXI. Motor Vehicles

Statutes are typically divided into Titles and Chapters.

Chapter 265-A Alcohol or Drug Impairment (Refs & Annos)

➡ Driving or Operating Under the Influence of Drugs or Liquor

265-A:2 Driving or Operating Under the Influence of Drugs or Liquor; Driving or Operating With Excess Alcohol Concentration

This is the specific name of the DUI statute.

(I) No person shall drive or attempt to drive a vehicle upon the ways of this state open to the public or operate or attempt to operate an OHRV:

(a) While such person is under the influence of intoxicating liquor or any controlled drug or any combination of intoxicating liquor and controlled drugs; or

(b) While such person has an alcohol concentration of 0.08 or more, or in the case of a person under the age of 21, 0.02 or more.

Note that the statute prohibits two types of conduct: "drive or attempt to drive a vehicle" and "operate or attempt to operate a boat."

(II) No person shall operate or attempt to operate a boat while under the influence of intoxicating liquor or a controlled drug or any combination of intoxicating liquor and a controlled drug or drugs, or while such person has an alcohol concentration of 0.08 or more, or in in the case of persons under the age of 21, 0.02 or more.

Updated with laws currently effective May 6, 2020 through Chapter 8 of the 2020 Reg. Sess., not including changes and corrections made by the State of Magnolia, Office of Legislative Services.

Under this statute, a person can commit DUI of a vehicle or a boat in two different ways. Under section (a), a person can be guilty of DUI if he or she is under the influence of alcohol or controlled drugs. Under section (b), a person violates the statute if the concentration of alcohol is over .08 or, in the case of someone under 21, more than .02.

Most statutes can be deconstructed into specific elements. One way to think about elements is to ask: "What must the government (or state) prove?" or, in a civil case, "What must a plaintiff prove?" Here, the statute requires that all four of the elements must be met, although there are alternative ways to meet the statute (e.g., boat or vehicle). This formulation—requiring several elements to be met—is called **conjunctive**. The formulation is called **disjunctive** when there are alternative ways to meet a statute. The Magnolia DUI statute is a good example of a law that incorporates both. To violate the statute, an individual must "drive or attempt to drive a vehicle upon the ways of this state open to the public or operate or attempt to operate an OHRV" AND either fit within subsection (a) OR subsection (b).

The "AND" represents a conjunctive portion of the statute, and the "OR" represents a disjunctive portion. When you are breaking down a statute and identifying what it requires, look for whether the elements are disjunctive or conjunctive.

Okay, let's break that down. To prove that Mr. Clover violated this statute, the prosecutor (the lawyer representing the State of Magnolia) must prove:

1. That Mr. Clover was driving or attempting to drive
2. A vehicle
3. Upon a way in Magnolia open to the public
4. Under the influence or with a BAC over 0.08.

Notice how each of these elements contains terms that may need further defining: "driving," "way," and perhaps "vehicle." State statutes include a definitional section. Usually, this section appears at the beginning of a particular title or chapter, or it can occur at the beginning of the entire statutory code. Part of understanding a statute includes checking if the legislature has defined particular words or phrases in the appropriate definitional section.

We will touch on "way" in Chapter 10.

At this point, you would want to return to the Supervising Attorney's memo to ensure you follow her instructions. She stated: "There is no question that the breathalyzer is correct, that Mr. Clover is an adult, and that Mr. Clover was intoxicated when he was found asleep in his car. The only issue that you should address is whether Mr. Clover was 'driving.'" From her instructions, we know we are focused on the driving element, for now.

> **PRACTICAL TIP**
>
> Many states have model jury instructions. These are templates that judges use when instructing a jury about what they must find in a particular case. A committee of state bar members and judges usually writes jury instructions. The instructions typically outline the elements of a crime (in a criminal case) or cause of action (in a civil case). They are usually available online or through the state's Bar association. This is a good resource to use in identifying elements.

HOW DO COURTS INTERPRET STATUTES?

Much of a lawyer's time is spent analyzing a court's interpretation of a statute. Courts follow some basic rules when they interpret and apply statutes. These are known as the Canons of Construction. Here is a brief description of the most widely used rules:

- *Plain Meaning Rule.* The court will look at the actual words of the statute and apply a common, ordinary meaning. Sometimes a court will use a dictionary definition of a common word to identify its meaning.
- *Legislative Intent.* The court will examine documents (e.g., hearing minutes, committee reports, or preambles) to discern the legislators' goals in drafting the statute. Sometimes a court will examine other parts of a statute, or the statute as a whole, to discover the legislative intent.
- *Stare Decisis.* The court may examine lower courts' interpretations of the statute or interpretations of similar statutes from other states.

After you understand the statute, the next step is to examine whether the statute applies to your facts. Is the statute a good fit, given your client's facts? What questions do you have about how it might apply? This inquiry will likely point you toward case law, and thus the next step is to read cases where the court has applied the statute's terms. In the case of Mr. Clover, we are interested in the meaning of the term, "drive" for now, and later, in Chapter 10, we will discuss the meaning of "way." The cases identified by your supervisor (and in the text below) focus on the meaning of "drive"—in each case the court is examining and applying whether the facts in the case come within the meaning of this term.

READING AND UNDERSTANDING CASES

Law students and lawyers must carefully read cases to gather information about a specific question or to learn about an area of law. As a law student, you may be preparing for class or, as in your legal writing class, answering a client's question. Lawyers similarly may read a case to learn updates in an area of law or with a client's question in mind. Either way, when you are reading a case, you are attempting to extract important information that will help you understand the landscape of the relevant law. One method to extract and note the information from case law is called briefing a case. You will brief cases to prepare for your class discussions (in all your law school classes), to understand an area of law, and to prepare to answer a legal question. Briefing is effective because it forces you to think about what the court did and why.

At first, your case briefs will follow a format suggested to you. As you progress through law school and legal employment, you will likely adapt your briefing format to a style that works for you. You may find that how you brief a case for your classes differs from how you brief cases you read for a research project. When you brief a case for your Torts or your Contracts class, you will brief the cases with a focus on preparing for your classroom discourse. When you brief a case relevant to a client's legal issue, you will create a brief focused on understanding a potential answer to your client's issue. Whatever your purpose, there is a universal briefing template. The template is a starting point for you to use as a tool, but you will undoubtedly find your own personal approach to briefing a case. We give you the basics here. At first, briefing a case will take you a long time. As you get used to it, the process will go faster, but don't try to rush through. Careful, almost forensic, reading and analysis are at the core of good lawyering.

When judges decide cases and write opinions, they do not operate in a world untethered from particular facts, precedent, or social policy. They may conform to past decisions, or they may decide to change old law. Every case is decided because a specific set of facts is before the court. And every case is decided within the social construct and norms existing when an opinion is written. Opinions are not always clear, and you may have to figure out what a court is saying by studying the opinion carefully and reading between the lines for implicit reasoning.

Sometimes the reasoning the court uses seems convoluted. This may be more likely to happen when the court wanted to reach a certain result and had to bend the reasoning to get there. Sometimes courts decide cases and give very little justification for the ruling. If you are confused by a court's opinion, don't automatically assume you are missing something. It might be that the reasoning or the holding is hard to discern. Law students are often surprised at how long it can take to read and comprehend even a short case. Reading a case usually means studying it—reading it repeatedly for a clear and accurate understanding.

> **PRACTICAL TIP**
>
> Most of the time you will read cases on screens. BE VERY CAREFUL that you read the court's *entire opinion* (the headnotes are not part of the opinion) all the way to the end. Do not skim or jump from page to page. Not reading the entire case, page by page, runs a potentially dangerous risk of missing a key point.

When you read cases online, be careful that you do not miss parts. Be sure to read *everything* the court says. For example, a court may begin a case by running through the facts. However, the holding (the decision the court makes on the question before it)—and remember that the holding will likely appear toward the end of the case—may only rely on one or two of these facts. To understand the holding, you must be sure that you understand the **decisive facts,** not just the overall facts of the case. The court may also acknowledge an important policy or societal concern at the end of an opinion or in the middle. Think of yourself as an investigator, because you need to comb through and identify all the key points in a case that help you solve your client's problem. Your case brief will help you keep track of those key points.

Decisive facts are the facts the court relied on to make its decision. These facts can often be found in the reasoning section of a case.

Why Brief Cases?

- Because briefing forces you to study the case and condense its most important information.
- Because briefing helps you organize the cases. This is especially true when your research project involves numerous cases.
- Because briefing helps you efficiently refer to cases as you write your memorandum.

General Tips on Briefing

- It will be time consuming at first. Have patience, because soon you will be briefing cases more quickly.
- Study cases you read for a research project like you study a case to prepare for a class. Re-read the case several times, highlighting and taking notes about your reading.
- Remember that the headnotes at the beginning of an opinion are not part of the opinion and are not written by the court.
- Resist the impulse to use a lot of quotes. Try to put the case information in your own words. This will help ensure that you understand what the court is saying.

Parts of a Case Brief

The list below provides the building blocks for a briefing template. These are the universal components of a case:

- Name, date, court
- Procedural history
- Facts
- Issue(s)
- Holding(s)
- Reasoning
- Disposition
- Comments/dicta

Parts of a Case Brief in Detail

Name of the Case, Date, Court

- Use *ALWD or Bluebook* form where possible. Be sure to note the date of the decision. Identify the level of the court the case comes from. Cross reference in the *Bluebook* tables to understand the hierarchy of courts if the case is from a state court.
- Understand the players.
- Plaintiff = person who brought the lawsuit
- Defendant = person being sued or charged criminally
- Appellant = person who lost in lower court and brings appeal
- Appellee = person who won below and responds to appeal
- Petitioner = person petitioning court to hear appeal
- Respondent = person responding to the appeal

Procedural History

- Identify what occurred in the lower court to cause this case to be in the appellate court. Usually, you can find this information at the beginning of the case.

Facts

- Include facts that give the case context.
- Include the decisive facts upon which the court's holding rests. These are often found at the end of the opinion where the court gives its holding.

Issue

- Identify the legal question the court is resolving. You can frame this as a question with a yes or no answer.

Holding

- This is the court's decision on the question that was actually before it.
- The holding directly answers the question presented in the issue. If the issue has more than one question, the opinion will contain a holding for each question.
- Characterize the parties to state the decision in its broadest terms. (Example: Instead of "Mr. Jones can sue . . . ," state the holding as "A father can sue. . . .")

Reasoning

- Identify the reasons given by the court for reaching its decision, including explicit and implicit reasoning.
- Identify what types of reasoning the court uses.
  - The reasoning explains why the court ruled the way it did.
  - Often the reasoning combines decisive facts and the legal issue.

Disposition

- Identify the action the court took.
- Did it reverse the lower court's ruling? Remand the case? Affirm the lower court's decision?
- Understand the key terms: reverse, remand, reconsideration, affirm.

The Rule

- Identify the rule from the case.
- Combine the holding and the reasoning to ascertain the rule.
- What is the general legal principle applicable to the particular factual circumstance that the case stands for?
- The rule may not be clearly stated, in which case you need to infer the rule by putting together the decisive facts, the holding, and the reasoning.

Comments/Dicta

- "Comments" are comments you might write to yourself about something you do not understand in the case or something that seems interesting or thought provoking that you want to ask about.
- "Dicta" is extra language in the opinion that is not part of the holding. It may touch upon a legal issue, but if it does not directly address the issue before the court, it is dicta and not law.
- Dicta might be in the form of a policy statement the court wants to make.
- Dicta can sometimes be a good indication of what the court may do in future cases.

Read through the *Holloran* case in Chapter 5 and create a brief of the case. Then compare your brief with the one below.

State v. Holloran, 140 M.G. 563 (1995).

Parties: State of New Hampshire (prosecutor) and Patrick Holloran (defendant)

Procedural History: Holloran was convicted after a bench trial in Derry District Court. Case appealed directly to Supreme Court.

Facts: Holloran was sitting alone in driver's seat of parked truck on Symmes Drive in Londonderry. Engine was not running but the keys were in the ignition. Officer "spotlighted" car, and Holloran "jumped out" and was "unsteady" on his feet. Holloran told the officer he was waiting for a call from his wife who was in another town at a Tupperware party. He indicated he would be picking her up at the end of the party. Holloran did not have a phone, but he did have a pager. According to officer, Holloran was glassy eyed, disheveled, and his breath smelled like alcohol. Holloran told the officer he had nothing to drink. He failed 3 sobriety tests and was arrested for DUI.

Issue: Whether when viewing the evidence in the light favorable to the State, a fact finder could find that Holloran was in actual physical control of his vehicle.

Holding: Yes, a person under these circumstances—who was sitting in the driver's seat with the keys in the ignition and who indicated he was waiting for a call to pick up another person in a nearby town—is in actual physical control of his vehicle.

Rule: Driving is defined as operating or having actual physical control. (564) Actual physical control is defined as "capacity bodily to guide or exercise dominion over the vehicle at the present time." (565) Primary focus is whether person is using car as a "stationary shelter" or will put the public in danger.

In the brief, indicate the page number so you can locate it later when you need it to write the citation in your memo.

Reasoning: Here, Holloran wasn't just "Parked While Intoxicated" and instead would "imminently operate" the car while intoxicated. (565)

Disposition: District Court decision affirmed. (Conviction stands.)

In Comments, you can indicate something you think is important about the case, something you want to remember, or a connection to your client's case.

Comments: Important policy of keeping public safe from danger or imminent danger.

Read and brief the *O'Malley* and *Winstead* cases. The briefs of both cases can be found in Appendix C.

STUDYING A CASE

Now that we have extracted and noted important information from the case in a brief, let's look at the parts of a case for clues in our investigation.

 Video Quiz

Breaking Down a Case

Below is the first case your Supervising Attorney attached to her Memorandum. You have already read through the case and briefed it. We will break the case down further here.

Identifying Parts of a Case: Citation, Caption, Date, Summary, and Headnotes

Let's take a look at the *Holloran* case. To start, look at the caption and the summary:

PRACTICAL TIP

In the appendix of your *ALWD* or *Bluebook* under "United States Jurisdictions" you will find the citation form for every state. These pages will also indicate to you what the court system is in a particular state and what each level of the court is called.

This is the case citation. State appellate cases are typically published in two reporters: a state reporter and a regional reporter. The first number is the reporter volume, and the second number is the page number where the first page of the case appears in the reporter.

These are the names of the parties. The state is a party because this is a criminal case brought against an individual.

This is the date the case was decided.

The first paragraph is a summary (also referred to as a synopsis) of the case that includes what happened procedurally. The summary is typically written by editors who work for the publisher, not the court, and thus, should not be cited. Even if the summary was written by a judge (e.g., Justice Ginsburg wrote her own summaries), it should not be cited because it is not part of the opinion.

140 M.G. 563, 669 A.2D 800

Supreme Court of Magnolia.

The STATE of Magnolia

v.

Patrick W. Holloran.

No. 94-558.

December 27, 2000.

Defendant was convicted before the Derry District Court, Rockingham County, Warhall, J., of driving under the influence, and he appealed. The Supreme Court held that evidence was sufficient to find that defendant was in actual physical control of his truck, as required by conviction, notwithstanding that truck was legally parked, its lights were off, and engine was not running.

WEST HEADNOTES

Automobiles 48A 🔑 **355(6)**

48A Automobiles

   48AVII Offenses

      48AVII(B) Prosecution

         48Ak355 Weight and Sufficiency of Evidence

            48Ak355(6) k. Driving While Intoxicated. Most Cited Cases

Evidence in prosecution for driving while intoxicated was sufficient to find that defendant was in actual physical control of truck in which he was found, not withstanding that truck was legally parked, its lights were off, and engine was not running; when officer came upon truck, defendant was in the driver's seat, keys were in the ignition, defendant exhibited signs of drunkenness, and told officer that he was waiting for a call to pick up his wife, who was in another town; rational trier of fact could find beyond a reasonable doubt that defendant would be imminently operating truck. RSA 259:24, 265:82.

**800 *563. Jeffrey R. Howard, Acting Atty. Gen. (Patrick E. Donovan, Assistant Attorney General, on the brief and orally), for State

*564 Casassa & Ryan, Hampton (Kenneth D. Murphy, on the brief and orally), for defendant.

**801 MEMORANDUM OPINION

PER CURIAM

After a bench trial, the Derry District (*Warhall, J.)* convicted the defendant, Patrick W. Holloran, of driving under the influence. *See* RSA 265:82, I (Supp. 1994). On appeal, the defendant asserts the trial court erred in denying his motion for a directed verdict based upon insufficiency of evidence. We affirm.

Side margin notes:

This "Headnote" is written by the publisher, West. Its purpose is to help with research and to quickly locate other sources under each topic. Because headnotes and the summary (above) are not written by the court and do not constitute the court's opinion, they should not be cited to or relied on as legal authority.

This is "star pagination." The double star tells you that this is the page number in the regional reporter. The single star refers to the page in the state reporter. Note the page numbers in your briefs so you will have the information for your citation when you start to write.

These are the names of the lawyers who wrote the briefs.

Per Curiam is a phrase indicating the court is not releasing who authored the opinion. Typically, the case would provide the judge or justice who wrote the opinion. For example, it might say "Broderick, J." This would indicate that Justice Broderick wrote the opinion. The "J" stands for judge or justice, not the first letter of the first name.

This is the beginning of the opinion, along with any dissent or concurrence, if one exists. The opinion is the only text you can rely on and cite to in your memorandum's analysis.

The Procedural History

The procedural history of the case explains what happened in the case before it came before the appellate court for review. Typically, the procedural history will include the particular issues the parties have raised for the appellate court's review. In the *Holloran* case, the procedural history is in the beginning of the case (the same paragraph as above).

From what the court describes, we know Mr. Holloran was found guilty of driving under the influence after a bench trial, a trial in front of a judge (in this case, Judge Warhall). Notice the court also identifies the issue on appeal: whether there was sufficient evidence to support the conviction. The court also directly answers the question raised in the issue in its statement: "We affirm," meaning that the court agreed with the lower court's decision. Many judicial opinions address more than one issue. Often, only one of these issues will be relevant to your problem. You should carefully read the whole case, but you will focus your study of the case on the particular issue that concerns the problem at hand. In Mr. Clover's case, that issue is the meaning of "driving" under the Magnolia statute. Thus, we will read the *Holloran* case looking to study the facts the court found to be sufficient for the driving element.

Distinguishing Background Case Facts Versus Decisive Case Facts

In the *Holloran* case above, what follows is the court's rendition of the case facts. These paragraphs appear in the beginning of the court's opinion:

In the evening of March 15, 1999, Londonderry Police Officer Mark Cagnetta approached a Chevrolet pickup truck with its lights off parked on Symmes Drive in Londonderry. The officer saw the defendant sitting alone behind the wheel. Cagnetta "spotlighted" the truck and the defendant quickly jumped out. Cagnetta told the defendant to get back into the truck, observing that the defendant appeared "unsteady" on his feet.

The defendant explained that he was waiting for a call from his wife to pick her up from a Tupperware party in Auburn. The officer did not see a phone, and the defendant indicated that he had a pager. Cagnetta noticed that the defendant's breath smelled of an alcoholic beverage, that his eyes were glassy and bloodshot, and that he appeared disheveled. The officer also observed that although the engine was not running, the keys to the truck were in the ignition. The defendant stated that he had been at the airport and had come to Symmes Drive to wait for his wife, but that he had had nothing to drink that evening and should have remained at the airport. After the defendant failed three field sobriety tests, Cagnetta arrested him for driving while under the influence of alcohol.

The following excerpt is where the court identifies the critical facts on which they based their holding. This appears at the end of the opinion:

> The defendant argues that because the truck was legally parked, the lights were off, and the engine was not running, it is speculative to conclude that he would soon be operating the vehicle. These acts alone, however, are not dispositive. When Officer Cagnetta came upon the truck, the defendant was in the driver's seat. The defendant **802 exhibited signs of drunkenness, and he told the officer that he was waiting for a call to pick up his wife, who was in another town. The keys were in the ignition. In the context of the officer's observations and the defendant's statements, a rational trier of fact could find beyond a reasonable doubt that the defendant was not merely Parked While Intoxicated but would be imminently operating the truck in an inebriated condition, and, therefore, that he was in actual physical control of the vehicle.

Notice that the court relies on only some of the facts to reach a conclusion about whether the defendant, Mr. Holloran, was in actual physical control of the truck because he would be imminently operating the vehicle. How do you know this? The court says the facts argued by the defendant are "not dispositive." Instead, the court highlights the defendant's statement that he was waiting to pick up his wife in another town and that the keys were in the ignition. The court is signaling to the reader that these are the facts that decided the defendant's status.

Why is it so important to know the *decisive* facts of the case? Because it will help you find the answer to your client's problem. Let's look at the facts of Mr. Clover's case. You have been asked to analyze whether he was "driving" under the Magnolia law. The *Holloran* case tells you certain indicia of control showed the defendant was driving—that the defendant had the keys in the ignition and that he made a statement about his intention to drive. In Mr. Clover's case, there are also indicia of control, though they may not be the same ones. This tells you that these indicia of Mr. Clover's control will likely be decisive in determining whether he was "driving." Once you have identified the critical facts of the opinion (or opinions), you can identify the critical facts of your client's case.

The opinion will contain background that gives context to the case. In *Holloran,* an example of a background, or context, fact is that the incident occurred "in the evening." The court does not mention this fact as contributing to its holding, but it gives the reader context for the case. If the case were a burglary instead of a DUI, the fact that it was evening could be a decisive fact. But in this case, the time does not affect the disposition.

Because courts often must resolve more than one issue, particular facts may be decisive for one issue, but background facts for another issue. For example, in *Winstead* (printed in Chapter 5), the court explains that the defendant's car was parked in a Wal-Mart parking lot. This fact is not relevant to the question of whether the defendant was driving, but it is relevant to the issue raised regarding equal protection:

The defendant next argues that his right to equal protection was violated because Officer Hallock testified that he does not typically disturb people parked in recreational vehicles (RVs) in the Wal-Mart parking lot. Thus, the defendant argues, he was treated differently because he was in a car. We conclude, however, that this issue was also not preserved for appellate review.

Identifying the Court's Reasoning (IRAC)

Most court opinions follow a structure. For each issue (and often courts are addressing more than one issue in an opinion), the opinion will begin by setting out the issue. Often, in conjunction with the issue, the court will set out a brief (one- or two-sentence) summary of the moving party's argument on the particular point.

This is typically followed by an explanation of the law that relates to the issue. Next, the court applies the law, as it has explained it, to the facts of the case before it. Finally, the court will conclude with the outcome of the case. Sometimes a court will begin with the conclusion on the issue, and then repeat the conclusion after the explanation of the law and the application to the facts. This structure is referred to as "IRAC"—Issue, Rule, Application, and Conclusion. In various forms, the IRAC structure is the time-worn method of reasoning through a legal problem.

Although many opinions follow the IRAC structure and include the elements described above, they do not always follow the structure or include all the IRAC elements. When you are studying a case, you may have to hunt for the elements.

Let's look at the court's reasoning in *Holloran*. Note that we will focus only on the part of the opinion that addresses the issue in our case—the meaning of "driving" under the Magnolia statute.

This part of the opinion starts with a restatement of the defendant's argument and what led to the appeal.

At the close of the State's case, the defendant moved for a directed verdict, arguing that the evidence was insufficient for a rational trier of fact to find, beyond a reasonable doubt, that he had driven his truck on the night of the arrest. The court denied the motion and found the defendant guilty, sentencing him to a fine, ninety-day license revocation, and mandatory attendance in an alcohol awareness program. This appeal followed.

Here, the court gives the overall rule on the meaning of "driving" in Magnolia.

This constitutes the Issue—the I in IRAC—or the specific legal question before the court.

The defendant was convicted of violating RSA 265-A:2. "The *actus reus* contemplated in RSA 265-A:2 is 'driv[ing]' a motor vehicle while under the influence of alcohol." *State v. Willard*, 139 M.G. 568, 570, 660 A.2d 1086, 1087 (1995). "Driv[ing]" has been defined as "operat[ing]" or being in "actual physical control" of a motor vehicle. RSA 259:24 (1993). Because the State does not allege that the defendant was operating his truck, the question before us is whether *565 a rational trier of fact, viewing the evidence most favorably to the State, could have found beyond a reasonable doubt that the defendant was in actual physical control of the truck.

"To have 'actual physical control' of a motor vehicle, one must have the capacity bodily to guide or exercise dominion over the vehicle at the present time." *Willard,* 139 M.G. at 571, 660 A.2d at 1088 (emphasis omitted). What constitutes "actual physical control" will vary depending upon the facts of the case, but "the primary focus of the inquiry is whether the person is merely using the vehicle as a stationary shelter or whether it is reasonable to assume that the person will, while under the influence, jeopardize the public by exercising some measure of control over the vehicle." *Atkinson v. State,* 331 M.G. 199, 627 A.2d 1019, 1028 (1993). Specifically, in *Atkinson,* the defendant was not in actual physical control of his vehicle when he was asleep in the driver's seat with keys in the ignition, engine off, in a legally parked motor vehicle because there was no circumstantial or other evidence that the defendant climbed into his vehicle, put the key in the ignition, and went to sleep. *Id.* at 1029. In interpreting the statute to avoid a "Parked While Intoxicated" crime, we stated:

> The legislature has the desire to prevent intoxicated individuals from posing a serious public risk with their vehicles. However, we do not believe the legislature meant to forbid those intoxicated individuals who emerge from a tavern at closing time on a cold winter night from merely entering their vehicles to seek shelter while they sleep off the effects of alcohol. As long as such individuals do not act to endanger themselves or others, they do not present the hazard to which the drunk driving statute is directed. While we wish to discourage intoxicated individuals from first testing their drunk driving skills before deciding to pull over, this should not prevent us from allowing people too drunk to drive, and prudent enough not to try to seek shelter in their legally parked cars.

Id. at 1025-26.

At trial, the State adduced only circumstantial evidence to prove that the defendant had "actual physical control" of his truck. "[C]ircumstantial evidence which excludes any other rational conclusion is sufficient to establish beyond a reasonable doubt the *actus reus* set out in a motor vehicle statute." *Willard,* 139 M.G. at 571, 660 A.2d at 1088 (quotation and ellipses omitted). In applying this standard "we examine each evidentiary item in the context of all the evidence, not in isolation." *State v. Bissonnette,* 138 M.G. 82, 85, 635 A.2d 468, 469 (1993). The defendant argues that because the truck was legally parked, the lights were off, and the engine was not running, it is speculative to conclude that he would soon be operating the vehicle. These acts alone, however, are not dispositive. When Officer Cagnetta came upon the truck, the defendant was in the driver's seat. The defendant **802 exhibited signs of drunkenness, and he told the officer that he was waiting for a call to pick up his wife, who was in another town. The keys were in the ignition. In the context of the officer's observations and the defendant's statements, a rational trier of fact could find beyond a reasonable doubt that the defendant was not merely Parked While Intoxicated but would be imminently operating the truck in an inebriated condition, and, therefore, that he was in actual physical control of the vehicle. *See Willard,* 139 M.G. at 571, 660 A.2d at 1088; *Atkinson,* 627 A.2d at 1029.

The court further explains the rule by illustrating the *Atkinson* case. Notice the court first briefly describes the facts from *Atkinson* and then gives the holding and the rationale for the holding.

Here, the court has compared and applied the facts from *Atkinson* to the facts of *Holloran* to give its first holding or answer to the legal question. The comparison is the A for application or analysis and the holding is the C for conclusion in IRAC.

IRAC is a basic structure. You will use it in your own legal writing, but with some variation, as the case you are working on dictates. Although the structure of legal writing is like a court opinion, because a lawyer has different goals than a judge you may use IRAC in a variety of ways. Lawyers often use a structure with the acronym CREAC. This stands for Conclusion, Rule, Explanation of the rule, Application of the rule, and Conclusion (yes, Conclusion is in there twice—more on this when we break down how to write an analysis). There are many variations of the acronym for legal writing structure, including TRAC (Thesis, Rule, Application, Conclusion), BaRac (Bold Assertion, Rule, Application, Conclusion), or CREXAC (Conclusion, Rule, Explanation of rule, Application, Conclusion). These are only a few, and your writing professor may have a preferred one to use as a teaching tool. Whatever specific structure you are directed to use, the purpose for using the structure and the general elements is similar.

To break it down, here is a more detailed way to imagine how the acronym IRAC works in the context of court opinions:

I: Issue: This can be either the overall issue that contains more than one issue, or the individual issue therein.

R: The rule section is broken down into the overall rule and the explanation of the rule with illustrations from the cases.

A: The application shows how the law applies to the case before the court.

C: The conclusion gives the holding.

Understanding How a Court Reasons

While IRAC is the structure a court typically uses to explain a decision, *how* it reaches a decision usually is based on one or several kinds of legal reasoning. Understanding how courts reason through a legal problem should help you reason through your own analysis. Lawyers, like judges, make different kinds of arguments and use different kinds of reasoning depending on the case. Four types of reasoning are summarized below. Note that there are more, and court opinions often contain a combination of two or more kinds of reasoning.

- *Reasoning based on precedent (akin to stare decisis).* A court will apply a rule to a set of facts to reach a conclusion by looking at prior cases with similar facts and recognizing how the rule was applied in the prior cases. The court will reach a similar conclusion because the facts of the prior cases are similar enough to warrant this outcome. To justify the conclusion, the court will need to show *why* the prior cases' facts are similar. A good example of this kind of reasoning is in the cases you read for the sample case file. Review the last two paragraphs of *Winstead* (printed in Chapter 5 and briefed in Appendix C). The court explicitly compares the facts from *Willard*, noting that the two cases have almost "indistinguishable" facts. In the next paragraph, the court justifies its conclusion by demonstrating precisely how the two fact patterns are similar. This is how the court reasoned.

The prior case's facts may also be so different that a new outcome is warranted in the present case. For example, if there had been a prior Magnolia case where the defendant was in the *passenger* seat asleep instead of in the driver's seat, the court would likely distinguish those facts, saying that they are so different from the facts of *Winstead*, where the defendant was in the driver's seat, that a different result is warranted. The court's reasoning in *Diaz* (page 28) also contains precedential reasoning. Notice how the court uses explicit comparisons to the cases it has described:

> Applying the above-mentioned principles and case law, we hold that the trial court correctly found as a matter of law that the defendants did not owe the plaintiffs a duty under the facts of this case. Unlike the cases cited by the parties, the crosswalk at the intersection in question was controlled by a "Don't Walk" signal. Nonetheless, the instant plaintiff chose to ignore it and proceed across the remainder of the intersection. Unlike *Sweet*, the plaintiff was not a youngster who relied on the directions of an adult. While we agree that *Sweet* is good law, we do not go as far as *Valdez* where it is implied that a duty would exist if the plaintiff interpreted the bus driver's gesture as something more than an indication that the driver would not move the bus until the plaintiff passed.

- **Reasoning based on interpretation.** Courts will also base a ruling on the language of a statute or regulation. This type of reasoning can be combined with precedent reasoning because often interpreting statutes requires defining particular words or phrases in statutes. Courts will look at past cases where the same or similar language has been interpreted. They will analyze the "plain meaning" and they may also review legislative history to discern the legislature's intent in writing the law. Sometimes courts will use the dictionary when interpreting the meaning of a word in a statute.

  Here is an example of interpretative reasoning in a case where the defendant was arrested for DUI while riding a motorized stand-up two-wheel. The defendant, a healthy 25-year-old man who was using the scooter recreationally, unsuccessfully argued that the scooter was not a "vehicle" and even if it was, his use of the scooter should have fallen within a "mobility enhancement" exception of the statute. Note how the court discusses the words of the statute, the sentence structure of the statute, and the legislative history of the statute:

> Defendant contends there was insufficient evidence of a violation of N.C. Gen.Stat. §20–138.1 because the motorized scooter he was riding cannot be considered a "vehicle" within the meaning of the statute. We disagree. . . . "Statutory interpretation properly begins with an examination of the plain words of the statute." *Correll v. Division of Social Services,* 332 N.C. 141, 144,

418 S.E.2d 232, 235 (1992). If the language of a statute is clear, then the Court must implement the statute according to the plain meaning of its terms. *Id.* In the instant case, defendant was riding a motorized scooter with two wheels arranged in tandem, and the exclusionary provisions for horses, bicycles, and lawnmowers under N.C. Gen.Stat. §20–138.1(e) have no application. Defendant's scooter does meet the definition of a "device in, upon, or by which any person or property is or may be transported or drawn upon a highway" under N.C. Gen.Stat. §20–4.01(49).

Defendant, nonetheless, argues that "mobility enhancement" should be construed broadly in light of the dearth of legal precedent concerning the definition of that term. We reject this construction for two reasons. First, although "mobility enhancement" is not specifically defined in the statute, its placement within the sentence discussing "mobility impairment" leads us to conclude that the two terms are closely related and contravenes ascribing the broad definition urged by defendant. Indeed, there is no evidence that defendant was using the scooter other than for strictly recreational purposes. Second, the exception for devices being used for "mobility enhancement" was added to the sentence concerning "mobility impairment" in 2001 as part of "An Act to Make Technical Corrections and Conforming Changes to the General Statutes as Recommended by the General Statutes Commission." *See* Act of Dec. 6, 2001, ch. 487, §51, 2001 N.C. Sess. Laws 2725, 2806 (codified at N.C. Gen.Stat. §20–4.01(49) (2003)). In a memorandum, the General Statutes Commission explained that "[t]his bill makes corrections of a *technical nature* to various sections of the General Statutes." Memorandum from the Gen. Statutes Comm'n to Sen. Fletcher L. Hartzell & Rep. Bill Culpepper, N.C. Gen. Assembly (Dec. 3, 2001)(on file with the North Carolina Supreme Court Library) (emphasis added). Therefore, adding the term "mobility enhancement" was a technical change that did not substantively expand the existing mobility impairment exception to the term "vehicle." (From *State v. Crow* 175 N.C.App. 119 (N.C. 2005).)

- ***Rule-based reasoning.*** When a rule is indisputable and requires no interpretation, there is little reasoning to be done. For example, a law imposing a 55-mile-per-hour speed limit is a clear, objective standard. If your client was accused of driving at 80-miles-per-hour, there would be no need to argue about whether he violated the speed limit (if in fact he was going 80). Instead, you would give the rule (or law) and give no reasoning. If, instead, your client was charged with violating a law that prohibited driving at an unreasonable speed, you would need to analyze for your reader what "unreasonable"' means by doing precedential or other kinds of reasoning. In Mr. Clover's case, the rule that a driver must have .08 or higher blood alcohol concentration (BAC) to be over the legal limit is a clear standard. If Mr. Clover's BAC was .12, there would be little analysis regarding the law on this point; you would simply state the legal standard as a fact. If, instead, the law was that a person is prohibited from driving in an impaired condition, you would have to analyze and explain the meaning of "impaired" by doing precedential or other types of reasoning.

- ***Reasoning based on policy.*** A court may derive its holding from legal authority, but it may also justify a holding based on social policy or standards. Review the last paragraph of the *Diaz* decision on page 28 and reprinted below. The court says that the question of a signaler's duty concerns matters of "legal and social policies." The court is explicitly considering social norms in determining an answer in the case. Societal or economic concerns are another way a court justifies a case's outcome.

> We agree that an injury is foreseeable here. But whether a legal duty exists involves **1234 ***802 more than just foreseeability of possible harm; it also involves legal and social policies. (*Swett,* 169 Ill. App. 3d 78, 119 Ill. Dec. 838, 523 N.E.2d 594.) Here, the magnitude of guarding against the injury and the consequence of placing that burden on the defendant weigh heavily in favor of finding no duty. An adult pedestrian with no obvious impairments should be held responsible for deciding whether gestures and directions given by a motorist can be safely followed. We simply do not believe that the instant bus driver's act of common courtesy should be transformed into a tort thereby giving the plaintiff license to proceed across an intersection against a warning light and without taking any precautions of her own.

Keep in mind that courts often start with rule-based, interpretive, or precedential reasoning rather than policy-based reasoning because a court's function is to decide the law (or rule).

 **Video Quiz**

CHAPTER 7

Synthesizing Rules and Identifying Decisive Facts

INTRODUCTION

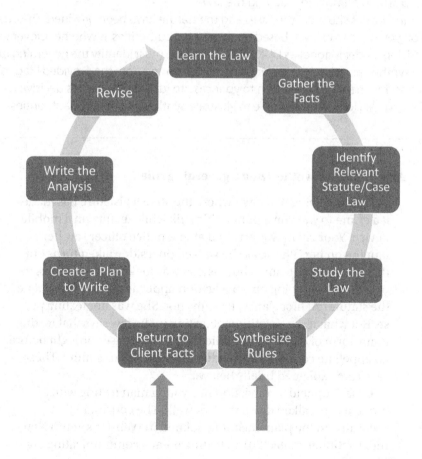

Now that you have read the relevant cases and statute for Mr. Clover's case, it is time to identify its governing rule. In the last chapter, we talked about reading and understanding the law. Once a lawyer has completed the research and gathered the legal authority needed to address the client's problem, the next step is to synthesize or pull together from the relevant sources an overall rule that governs the client's case. In this chapter, we first examine the process of synthesizing a governing rule using an example. We then synthesize a governing rule for our client, Mr. Clover's, case. The governing rule in your client's case will be included in the memo's roadmap paragraph, covered in Chapter 9.

As discussed in Chapter 6, a statute can form the basis of a rule that will guide a lawyer in solving a client's problem. However, interpreting the statute's meaning, specific terms in the statute, and how the statute applies to a client requires going beyond the statute and involves reading cases that address the statute. If no statute applies, then the rule or rules will only come from cases. Putting together slightly disparate principles to form one consolidated principle, or synthesized rule, that governs a client's problem is the next step after reading and studying the law.

In Clover's situation, the cases and the statute have been provided. The question you need to answer, based on those legal authorities, is whether Clover was "driving" under Magnolia's DUI law. To do so, you must identify the governing rule by synthesizing the decisive facts and the reasoning from the provided Magnolia authority. Then, you will return to your case to identify the client's decisive facts. First, we will look at an example to illustrate synthesis of multiple authorities.

An example of synthesizing a governing rule

Imagine living in a town where the state legislature has made it a crime to walk on a public sidewalk while texting on a mobile device. Your client was arrested after a police officer saw her tapping on her iPhone as she walked on a sidewalk. It turns out that she was not texting, but instead was looking at directions to where she was going on a navigation application. Did she violate the statute? At first glance, it seems not. She was not texting per se. But what if the definition of texting in the law says that texting is any form of digital communication? Three cases brought before an appellate court in the jurisdiction address this statute. These cases are explained briefly below.

Case A upheld a conviction of a young man texting with a friend as he walked down the sidewalk. The court said that according to the plain meaning defined in Webster's Tenth New Int'l Dictionary 2584 (2012), texting means communicating digitally with another by text messaging. Because the young man was engaged in a digital communication with another person, the court held he was texting, which was a clear violation of the statute.

Case B reversed the conviction of a young woman playing an interactive game on her smartphone as she walked down the sidewalk. The court justified its ruling by explaining that the law prohibited texting that amounts to interactive digital communication; because playing a game does not require communication with another, there was no violation.

Case C upheld a conviction of a man using a smartphone to write an email to another person while walking down the sidewalk. The court reasoned that emailing fits within the definition of digital communication because it involves communicating with another person, and the statute does not make an exception for communication that is not contemporaneous.

How do we reconcile the statute and the three cases to synthesize a governing rule that will apply to our client's case? First, we should consider the decisive facts, the holdings, and the reasoning in each case. Then we should consider a rule that reconciles the outcome of each case. The chart below outlines these parts for Cases A, B, and C.

	Case A	Case B	Case C	Synthesis = reconciliation of three cases
Decisive facts	D texting with a friend.	D playing a game on a smartphone.	D emailing on a smartphone.	Putting together the three cases, we get: A person violates the statute when they are communicating digitally with another individual.
Holding	Statute violated.	Statute not violated.	Statute violated.	
Reasoning	D is engaged in digital communication with another.	D is not engaged in interactive digital communication.	D engaged in communication with another even though it was not contemporaneous.	

Here, each of the cases addresses pedestrians who are walking while doing something on their phones. As you can see from the chart, the defendants violated the statute in Case A and Case C because they were texting with a friend and emailing another individual, respectively. In Case B, however, the pedestrian is not communicating with another person through her phone, only playing a game. The courts' implicit reasoning in the cases is that unless conduct involves digital communication with another, it does not violate the statute. In looking at the holdings, decisive facts, and implicit and explicit reasoning in these cases then, there is a statutory violation only if the defendants' conduct on their phone *involves actual communication with another individual.* This aspect—actual communication with another individual—is the commonality that allows us to synthesize a rule from the specific facts, holding, and reasoning in Cases A, B, and C.

The synthesized rule is essentially the governing rule in the client's case.

An example of the synthesized rule which starts with restating the statute:

> Under the state statute, texting on a mobile device while walking on a public sidewalk is a violation. Cite statute. The court has interpreted texting to require communication with another individual. Cite Cases A & C. Interacting with a smartphone in a manner that does not involve communication with another does not violate the statute. Cite Case B.

Identifying the Court's Reasoning. The decisions summarized in the example mainly rely on implicit reasoning for their decisions. However, when courts decide cases, they will often specifically explain *why* the decision is justified. Assume now that the courts have articulated, in addition, the reasoning in the chart below involving safety and policy justifications for each of their rulings.

	Case A	Case B	Case C	Synthesis + Common Reasoning
Decisive facts	D texting with a friend.	D playing a game on a smartphone.	D emailing on a smartphone.	Putting together the three cases, we get:
Holding	Statute violated.	Statute not violated.	Statute violated.	A person violates the statute when communicating digitally with another individual.
Reasoning	D is engaged in digital communication with another.	D is not engaged in interactive communication.	D engaged in communication with another even though it is not contemporaneous.	

	Case A	Case B	Case C	Synthesis + Common Reasoning
Reasoning (cont'd)	The underlying reason for the law is safety of citizens walking on the street.	Interactive communication with another individual on a smartphone is more distracting than simply using the phone while walking.	There are safety concerns inherent in distracted pedestrians engaged in digital communication with another individual, whether the communication is contemporaneous or not.	Common reasoning: Court is concerned about safety of pedestrians. An individual digitally interacting with another on a smartphone poses a greater danger than someone simply using the phone while walking.

The new synthesized rule together with the additional reasoning would look like this:

Under the state statute, texting on a mobile device while walking on a public sidewalk is a violation. Cite statute. The court has interpreted texting to require digital communication with another individual, an inherently distracting cell phone use that endangers public safety. Cite Cases A & C. However, use that does not involve digital communication with another is not a statutory violation because it is less distracting to the user and, thus, safer. Cite Case B.

This rule starts with the statute, the broadest rule. Overall, the rule explains when someone violates the statute and when someone does not. Thus it lays out the parameters of conduct prohibited under the statute, a reasonable way to approach synthesis when possible.

PRACTICAL TIP

We are providing two examples of the synthesized rule in the texting while walking example to show that synthesizing a rule requires careful examination of the language in the case law. Pay close attention to the decisive facts, the holdings, and the reasoning in each of the cases you are synthesizing. Reading and analyzing these carefully will help you articulate the governing principles, or synthesized rule, for your client's case.

Based on our articulated rules, our client's conduct does not seem to violate the statute. Our client was not engaged in communication with another individual. She was using a resource on her phone to get directions. Therefore, you can predict that she likely did not violate the statute.

Synthesizing the law and reconciling legal principles from several authorities is at the heart of what lawyers do. By studying relevant authorities carefully, a lawyer can interpret and apply a body of law to a client's problem. How well you can predict or argue a solution to a client's problem will depend on how well you have understood and synthesized the relevant law.

> **PRACTICAL TIP**
>
> Sometimes there is not much synthesis needed. If several cases simply restate the same rule and then apply it, you may not need to synthesize a rule. Instead, you will use the rule that is restated in the case law in your client's case. While courts can modify rules as each new fact scenario comes before the court, this is not always the case. Sometimes the outcome of a case leads to little change in the law or the rule applied.

Identifying Decisive Facts in a Client's Case

You must also identify the decisive facts in your client's case to write the memo for your supervising attorney. Synthesizing the governing rule and making a case chart will help you do this. Remember that in a court's opinion there are background facts and decisive facts; decisive facts are legally significant facts that affect the outcome of the case. The same is true of your client's case. You must first study the law and determine the decisive facts from the cases. Once you know this information, you can identify the decisive facts in your client's case.

In the synthesis example above, the legally significant facts of our client's case are that she was engaged in looking at directions on her phone and was not communicating with another individual. If the facts of our client's case had included that it was a sunny day, or that the client was a tourist from Europe, these facts would not affect the case's outcome. Those facts would be background facts, not decisive facts. The synthesized rule we came up with from Cases A, B, and C helped us to identify the critical fact that led to the courts' decisions, whether the defendant communicated with another.

The fact that our client was looking at directions and not communicating with another person leads to a probable outcome. She likely was not violating the statute. Thus, if the client came to us for advice, such as asking whether she should plead guilty or go to trial to fight the charge, we would advise that she likely has a good argument that she was not violating the statute and, therefore, may wish to fight the charge.

Synthesizing a Rule in Mr. Clover's Case

To answer the legal question in Mr. Clover's case, whether he was "driving" under Magnolia law, you must synthesize the governing rule from the statute and the case law. As noted, that synthesized rule will be incorporated into the roadmap paragraph of the discussion section of the memo you are writing for your supervising attorney.

To synthesize a governing rule in Mr. Clover's case, you should use a similar approach to that illustrated with the texting example. The chart below includes the decisive facts, the holdings, and the reasoning in the *Winstead*,

Holloran, and *O'Malley* cases. These cases are more complex than the texting example cases. However, the important pieces of the analysis can still be distilled to identify commonalities in the case law to help you determine the governing rule for "driving" under Magnolia law.

	Winstead	*Holloran*	*O'Malley*	**Synthesis**
Decisive facts	D found asleep in the driver's seat of a car in a parking lot Engine running Before falling asleep, D unlocked door, sat in driver's seat, pushed clutch in, moved gear shift to neutral, started engine, and turned on heater	D awake, sitting in driver's seat of truck parked legally, waiting for call from wife to pick her up from a party Engine off & lights off Keys in ignition	D had no intent to operate and did not operate vehicle D went out to friend's vehicle to start it so friend could give him a ride home D fell asleep in vehicle D found asleep in driver's seat Keys in ignition & engine off	
Holding	D driving	D driving	D not driving	The court considers circumstantial evidence such as D's actions, the status of the vehicle (e.g., whether engine on or off), and D's statements/intent to decide if D was driving. This type of circumstantial evidence is indicia of control and establishes actual physical control (or not).
Reasoning	APC = "capacity bodily to guide or exercise dominion over a vehicle at the present time." Circumstantial evidence can establish APC The circumstantial evidence (listed under decisive facts) shows that "a rational trier of fact could find beyond a reasonable doubt that D was in APC of the car before he fell asleep."	Court explains being "Parked While Intoxicated" may not be enough for APC under the statute, but here there is enough. Circumstantial evidence can establish APC Facts that support APC: D in driver's seat of truck, keys in ignition, waiting for a call to pick up his wife Based on this evidence a rational trier of fact could conclude that D would "imminently operat[e]" the vehicle. Thus, in APC.	Circumstantial evidence can establish APC beyond a reasonable doubt (BRD) Facts including D's testimony (under decisive facts) not contradicted by State In absence of evidence BRD that D drove or would imminently operate the vehicle, his mere presence in a nonmoving vehicle is insufficient to establish APC.	

Let's examine a bit more closely how we chose the information from the cases to include in the case chart. We will use the *Winstead* case as an example, but you could do a similar analysis of each of the cases to decide what to include in your case chart. As discussed in Chapter 6, the court will rely on the decisive facts in the case when deciding if the defendant was driving or in actual physical control of the vehicle. Just like we identified the key paragraph in the *Holloran* case in Chapter 6, the key reasoning paragraphs in the *Winstead* case are at the end of the opinion and identify the decisive facts on which the court based its holding. They are reprinted below.

> "To have 'actual physical control' of a motor vehicle, one must have the capacity bodily to guide or exercise dominion over the vehicle at the present time." *State v. Willard,* 139 M.G. 568, 571, 660 A.2d 1086 (1995) (emphasis omitted). Circumstantial evidence of imminent operation is also sufficient for actual physical control. *See id.* Accordingly, while a person who is sound asleep cannot have such a capacity, "circumstantial evidence which excludes any other rational conclusion is sufficient . . . to establish beyond a reasonable doubt the *actus reus* set out in a motor vehicle statute." *Id.* (quotation omitted).
>
> This case is indistinguishable from *Willard*. In *Willard*, the defendant was found asleep in the driver's seat of his vehicle in a parking lot with the vehicle's engine idling. A police officer woke him, determined he was intoxicated and arrested him for driving while intoxicated. In holding that *248 a rational trier of fact could find that the defendant was in *actual physical control* of the vehicle, we noted that "if circumstantial evidence were to prove that [the] defendant [ ] started his car before falling asleep, he would have been in actual physical control of it while awake and in the driver's seat." *Id.*; see also *Atkinson v. State,* 331 M.G. 199, 627 A.2d 1019, 1028 (1993) ("Indeed, once an individual has started the vehicle, he or she has come as close as possible to actually [operating it] without doing so and will generally be in 'actual physical control' of the vehicle.").
>
> Here, the defendant was also found asleep in the driver's seat of a car in a parking lot with the engine running. Moreover, the defendant testified at trial that he unlocked the door, sat in the driver's seat, pushed the clutch in, moved the gear selector to neutral, started the engine and turned on the heater. Given these facts and the reasonable inferences therefrom, a rational trier of fact could find beyond a reasonable doubt that the defendant was in actual physical control of the car before he fell asleep. *See Willard,* 139 M.G. at 571, 660 A.2d 1086.

Just like in the *Holloran* case, where the court relied on the indicia of control over the vehicle to conclude the defendant was in actual physical control of the vehicle, the court in *Winstead* similarly relied on indicia of control over the vehicle to determine the defendant was in actual physical control. In *Winstead*, the control occurred before the defendant fell asleep. In *Holloran* the key evidence concerned intent to drive imminently. Regardless, the decisive facts involved capacity and either past control over the vehicle or imminent intent to control the vehicle. As you can see from studying the case chart for *Winstead*, and comparing it to the text of the case, the decisive facts and the court's reasoning are laid out in the last paragraphs of the case. As a result, when you are reading and briefing your cases, make sure to identify where in the decision the court focuses on the reasoning and holding for the issue relevant to your client's case. The reasoning will help you identify decisive facts and, in turn, help you synthesize the governing rule in your client's case in conjunction with the other relevant authorities. This type of careful analysis will also lead you to identify the decisive facts in your client's case.

The Synthesized Rule in Mr. Clover's Case

Below is an example of one way to write the synthesized rule in Mr. Clover's case. It is based on the language of the Magnolia DUI statute and a synthesis of the decisive facts, holdings, and reasoning in the *Winstead*, *Holloran*, and *O'Malley* cases.

> A person violates the Magnolia DUI statute if they "drive or attempt to drive a vehicle upon the ways of this state open to the public" while they are under the influence of drugs or alcohol. M.G. Rev. Stat. Ann. § 265-A:2 (2022). To meet the statute, three elements must be proved: (1) driving or attempting to drive; (2) on a way; and (3) under the influence. § 265-A:2. Driving is defined as operation or being in "actual physical control" of the vehicle. *State v. Holloran*, 669 A.2d 800, 801 (M.G. 1995). The state can prove "actual physical control" if there is circumstantial evidence that the defendant had "the capacity bodily to guide or exercise dominion over the vehicle at the present time" before falling asleep, or that the defendant would "imminent[ly] operate" the vehicle. *State v. Winstead*, 836 A.2d 775, 778 (M.G. 2003); see also *Holloran*, 669 A.2d at 801-02. *But see State v. O'Malley*, 416 A.2d 1387, 1388 (M.G. 2002). "Actual physical control" differentiates between one using a vehicle as a shelter, and one who presents a public safety risk by exercising control of the vehicle while inebriated. *Holloran*, 669 A.2d at 801.

This part of the rule is from the statute.

The rest of the synthesized rule comes from definitions and an examination of the decisive facts, holdings, and reasoning in the case law.

Because we are only addressing 1 issue, the issue of "driving," we can provide all the rules in 1 main roadmap paragraph. If we were addressing more than 1 issue, e.g., whether Mr. Clover was driving and whether he was driving on a way, then we would separate out the overall rules, and the rules for each issue under appropriate headings. You will read more about this in Chapter 10.

When you read the sample memo for the driving issue in Chapter 8, you will see all the pieces of the above rule included in the roadmap paragraph in the memo (in addition to other pieces often included in a roadmap). This synthesized, governing rule laid out in the roadmap is the foundation upon which the rest of the discussion section will build.

 **VIDEO QUIZ**

IDENTIFYING CLIENT FACTS

Now that you have carefully read and studied the law and identified the synthesized, governing rule, you need to return to the client facts and identify which are decisive. You must take this step to prepare to write the discussion section of your memo. Identifying the decisive facts of your client's case goes together with understanding the governing synthesized rule, and the reasoning behind the governing rule. You won't know which of your client's facts are legally relevant until you know the governing rule.

You will be using the CREAC structure to write the discussion section. While the CREAC structure will be discussed in more detail in Chapter 10, as explained previously, CREAC stands for Conclusion, Rule, Explanation of the rule, Application of the rule, and Conclusion. You have used the case chart to synthesize the R in CREAC (the governing rule). The decisive facts, holding, and reasoning from the cases in the case charts provides the basis of the E in your discussion section. Now returning to the client facts will help you identify which client facts to include in the A of your CREAC, the part of your memo where you will apply the law to the client facts to reach a prediction.

Reprinted below is a partial case chart. (For simplicity, we have reprinted only a portion of the case chart that includes the decisive facts and holdings from the cases.) Instead of a synthesis column, it includes a client facts column to aid in planning the A in CREAC. Complete the online exercise below to fill in the client facts column for Mr. Clover's case.

 VIDEO QUIZ

Let's turn to Clover's case. From the three cases and the synthesized rule above, you know that the court's decisions all turn on indicia of a defendant's control over a car. To identify the decisive facts from Clover's case, look for facts that could establish indicia of control over the car. You should also consider if there are any facts that might weigh against control.

Include here the decisive facts in your client's case that you identified by examining the case law. Which facts did the courts rely upon in the reasoning? Your prediction will use the same types of facts as determinative facts from the client's case. After writing in client facts for Mr. Clover's case, compare your work to the completed chart in Appendix C.

	Winstead	Holloran	O'Malley	Client facts
Decisive facts	D found asleep in the driver's seat of a car in a parking lot Engine running Before falling asleep, D unlocked door, sat in driver's seat, pushed clutch in, moved gear shift to neutral, started engine, and turned-on heater	D awake, sitting in driver's seat of truck parked legally, waiting for call from wife to pick her up from a party Engine off & lights off Keys in ignition	D had no intent to operate and did not operate vehicle D went out to friend's vehicle to start it so friend could give him a ride home D fell asleep in vehicle D found asleep in driver's seat Keys in ignition & engine off	
Holding	D driving	D driving	D not driving	

CHAPTER 8

Overview of the Office Memorandum

INTRODUCTION

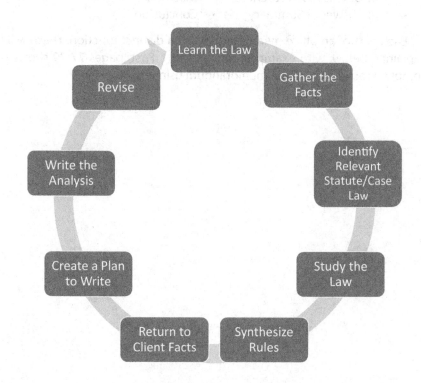

When your research is done, and you have closely read and studied the law, you will begin on the steps for writing an interoffice memorandum. In the last chapter, we reviewed how to identify rules from case law and how to synthesize the rules from individual cases into one rule that can be applied to your client's problem. You have also used what you learned from the case law to identify the decisive facts in your client's case. Now, you will begin writing beyond the rules of your case. You may be used to writing a document from beginning to end. However, in legal writing, we typically draft our Issue, which guides our discussion section, and then go back to write the facts and summary sections. Writing the discussion section helps narrow the facts and summary sections of the memorandum.

In the next chapter, we will discuss "planning to write." In this chapter, we will take a brief detour from the steps on the wheel above to provide and explain a sample memorandum on Mr. Clover's legal issue.

SAMPLE MEMORANDUM

The parts of a typical interoffice memorandum include:

- Heading
- Issue or Question Presented
- Brief Answer or Summary
- Facts
- Discussion
- Conclusion

Each part of an office memorandum has a distinct function. These will be explained below, with examples for each part. First, pages 77-79 shows is a complete sample one-issue memorandum using our case file.

MEMORANDUM

To: Supervising Attorney

From: Student Associate

Date: July X, 20XX

Re: Cleo Clover's DUI arrest – sufficiency of evidence for driving element

ISSUE

Under Magnolia Driving Under the Influence (DUI) law, did Mr. Clover "drive" on a way when he was found sleeping in the driver's seat of his car with the accessories in use but the engine off?

SUMMARY

Likely yes. For purposes of Magnolia's DUI law, Mr. Clover was likely "driving" on a way. Under the Magnolia DUI statute, Mr. Clover must drive on a way while under the influence of drugs or alcohol. There is no question that Mr. Clover was under the influence. Further, Mr. Clover drove because he had actual physical control of his car when he ignited the accessories in the vehicle while positioned in the driver's seat coming as close as possible to driving.

FACTS

Mr. Clover is a software engineer who lives in Sweetwater, Magnolia. On Friday, October X, 20XX, at 2:00 a.m. Sweetwater Police Officer Lena Starling patrolled an apartment complex when she saw a car parked in a reserved space with the lights on and someone seated in the driver's seat. Upon closer inspection, the person was asleep with his head back in the driver's seat. Mr. Clover responded after Officer Starling knocked on his window twice, one time forcefully.

When Mr. Clover put his window down, Officer Starling detected an odor of alcohol and further observed that Mr. Clover's eyes were bloodshot and that he appeared dazed. Officer Starling identified Mr. Clover through his license and registration and asked why he was sleeping in his car. Mr. Clover admitted he had been at an office party that ended sometime after midnight. Because he thought he was impaired, he asked his co-worker, Robin Branch, to drive him to her apartment where he could safely leave his car and walk or take an Uber the rest of the way home. He told Officer Starling he was worried someone might come and tow his car, so he stayed to "sleep it off."

Mr. Clover explained in an interview that Branch drove his car to her apartment complex and pulled into the paved parking lot right off the main road. An automatic arm gate existed at the entrance to the parking lot, but Branch indicated it was broken and had been stuck in the "up" position for the past year. As a result, visitors to residents of the complex frequently parked in the lot. A sign, however, did indicate parking was for residents only and that all others would be towed.

Both Branch and Mr. Clover got out of the car. Branch gave Mr. Clover his key fob and went into her building. As it was a chilly fall night, Mr. Clover put the key fob in his pocket and got back in the driver's seat of his car so he could be warm while accessing his Uber app on his phone. Once inside he pressed the ignition button without pressing the brake to heat the car. Although the engine was not on, the car lights and heat were running. The car, a 2021 Toyota Highlander, turns on—the

---

Note the level of detail. The heading must clearly identify the subject.

Label each section of the Memo.

The Issue has three parts: (1) the controlling law—the Magnolia DUI statute, (2) the specific legal question, and (3) decisive facts that concern the legal question, whether Mr. Clover "drove" under the particular circumstance described.

The summary begins with a direct answer to the question set out in the issue and includes the level of certainty.

Then the summary includes the overall law and your conclusion, which weaves together subrules (e.g., actual physical control) and decisive facts.

The facts should include background or contextual facts as well as the decisive facts.

engine ignites—only if the key is nearby, and an occupant pushes the ignition button and brake simultaneously. Otherwise with only a push of the ignition button (without pressing the brake), the occupant can use the accessories. Once the heat was on, Mr. Clover leaned his head back and fell asleep before he completed the call for an Uber as navigating the app took longer than he wished due to poor cell service. Mr. Clover woke to Officer Starling's knocking.

When Officer Starling awoke and identified Mr. Clover, she asked Mr. Clover to exit the car and complete three field sobriety tests. Mr. Clover failed these tests. Mr. Clover explained to Officer Starling that he fell asleep after giving up on summoning an Uber and that he figured he could move the car if the person whose spot he was in returned. Officer Starling placed Mr. Clover under arrest. At the station, Mr. Clover was given a blood test which showed his BAC at .11.

The State of Magnolia charged Mr. Clover with Driving Under the Influence and now he seeks our advice as to whether the State can prove its case against him.

DISCUSSION

Mr. Clover was likely driving a vehicle under Magnolia's DUI statute because he was seated in the driver's seat with the key fob in his pocket, the car lights and heat turned on, prepared to drive. A person violates the Magnolia DUI statute if they "drive or attempt to drive a vehicle upon the ways of this state open to the public" while they are under the influence of drugs or alcohol. M.G. Rev. Stat. Ann. § 265-A:2 (2022). To meet the statute, three elements must be proved: (1) driving or attempting to drive; (2) on a way; and (3) under the influence. § 265-A:2. As Mr. Clover does not contest that he was under the influence, and another Associate is addressing whether he was on a "way," this memo will focus only on whether he was "driving." Driving is defined as operation or being in "actual physical control" of the vehicle. *State v. Holloran*, 669 A.2d 800, 801 (M.G. 1995). The state can prove "actual physical control" if there is circumstantial evidence that the defendant had "the capacity bodily to guide or exercise dominion over the vehicle at the present time" before falling asleep, or that the defendant would "imminent[ly] operate" the vehicle. *State v. Winstead*, 836 A.2d 775, 778 (M.G. 2003); see also *Holloran*, 669 A.2d at 801-02. *But see State v. O'Malley*, 416 A.2d 1387, 1388 (M.G. 2002). "Actual physical control" differentiates between one using a vehicle as a shelter, and one who presents a public safety risk by exercising control of the vehicle while inebriated. *Holloran*, 669 A.2d at 801.

To prove actual physical control, the driver must have the capacity bodily to guide or exercise control over the vehicle. *Winstead*, 836 A.2d at 778. In *Winstead*, the police find the defendant asleep and intoxicated upright in the driver's seat of his car, engine running, in a Wal-Mart parking lot. *Id.* at 776. The defendant testified that before falling asleep, he had unlocked the driver's side door, sat down, pressed the clutch, moved the car into neutral, started the engine, and turned on the heater. *Id.* at 778. Given the steps taken, and that starting the car comes "as close as possible" to operation, the court held that the defendant was in actual physical control of his vehicle before falling asleep. *Id.* (citing *Atkinson v. State*, 331 M.G. 199, 201 (M.G. 1993)).

Mr. Clover did exercise control over the vehicle because although the engine was not running, he took steps to put his body in a position to drive. Like the defendant in *Winstead* who testified to unlocking his car, pushing in the clutch, shifting to

---

Add a transition sentence before you start your legal analysis.

This is the Main Roadmap paragraph. It begins with your overall conclusion. Then it provides the relevant rules from broad to narrow (e.g., from the DUI statute to the driving element).

Dispense with any elements you are not addressing and why.

Because we are only addressing one issue, the issue of "driving," we can provide all the rules in one main roadmap paragraph. See Chapter 10 for information on memos addressing more than one issue, specifically separating the overall rules and the rules for each issue.

This is a Rule Explanation (RE) paragraph. It begins with one statement of law, already described in the roadmap paragraph but needing further explanation. Here Winstead's facts, holding and reasoning illustrate the statement of law.

This is a Rule Application (RA) paragraph. It corresponds to the RE paragraph above, and thus, starts with a conclusion on the rule explained in the RE paragraph.

neutral, and turning the engine on to have the heat running, Mr. Clover fell asleep in the seated position, lights and heat running. Mr. Clover unlocked and entered his car with his key fob nearby, pushed the ignition button, and turned on the heat. Even though igniting the engine would take the extra step of pushing in the brake, Mr. Clover, like the defendant in *Winstead*, came as close to operation of the vehicle as possible by seating himself in the ready position and igniting the accessories with the key fob before he fell asleep. Thus, Mr. Clover exercised control over the car and, as a result, was in actual physical control of the vehicle.

Additionally, the state can use circumstantial evidence to show the driver will imminently operate the vehicle to prove actual physical control. *Winstead*, 836 A.2d at 778. For example, in *Holloran*, the defendant legally parked his truck on the side of the road, alone in the driver's seat with keys in the ignition. 669 A.2d at 800. Although the engine was off, the defendant stated that he was waiting for a call from his wife to pick her up with the keys in the ignition, and these statements of intent to drive resulted in more than being "Parked While Intoxicated." *Id.* at 801. Instead, these facts show circumstantial evidence of imminent operation, and thus, the defendant presented "the hazard to which the drunk driving statute is directed" and was in actual physical control of his motor vehicle. *Id.*

Conversely, in *O'Malley*, the police found the defendant asleep in the driver's seat of a friend's car, with the keys in the ignition, legally parked outside the friend's house. 416 A.2d at 1388. The defendant testified that he had hitchhiked to the friend's house. *Id.* The friend agreed to drive the defendant home and told him to go "warm up" the car. *Id.* Finding this testimony "not unreasonable," the court held that there was not enough evidence to show imminent operation because "mere presence in a nonmoving vehicle" is insufficient to establish actual physical control. *Id.*

Mr. Clover was in actual physical control of his car because he declared his intention to move the vehicle. Like in *Holloran*, where the defendant's intention to pick up his wife in a neighboring town was enough to show actual physical control, Mr. Clover also indicated his intent to move the car should the resident whose spot he was in arrive home. Similar to *Holloran*, although Mr. Clover's engine was off, his decision to remain in the vehicle without calling an Uber and his statement of intent to drive, even conditionally, is circumstantial evidence of imminent operation. However, unlike in *O'Malley*, where the defendant was warming up the car so a friend could drive him home, Mr. Clover did not call an Uber or describe an alternative person or plan other than his intent to operate his vehicle. Even though Mr. Clover intended to "sleep it off" before he drove home, there is the possibility he would have to operate the vehicle while drunk, thereby presenting the type of "hazard" the drunk driving statute is trying to prevent. Mr. Clover's statement of imminent operation is more than being "Parked While Intoxicated" and thus, he likely had actual physical control over his vehicle.

CONCLUSION

Mr. Clover was likely driving as he was seated in the driver's seat with the keys in the ignition, and he indicated he would imminently operate his car.

The RA shows the analysis by making direct comparisons between the case illustrated and the client's case.

The reasoning from the precedent case, *Winstead*, is used to support the conclusion in the client's case.

The second RE paragraph begins with a new rule statement followed by two case illustrations to explain the rule.

Note the use of a transition word (conversely) to indicate that the author is still explaining the same rule and to identify the relationship between this case illustration (*O'Malley*) and the last one (*Holloran*).

This is the start of the second RA and corresponds to the second RE paragraph. It starts with a conclusion on the rule explained above and compares both cases illustrated.

Again, reasoning from the precedent case is used to support the conclusion.

The conclusion is a brief restatement of the overall conclusion.

SUGGESTED MEMORANDUM DRAFTING ORDER

As mentioned above, although the complete memorandum begins with the Issue, Brief Answer, and Facts sections, typically, you will write your interoffice memo in this order:

Draft an issue. At the beginning of your process, you identified the issue or the client's question or problem within an area of law. Now that you have studied the law, you can revise your issue and continue to revise it as you proceed in the writing process. Start by writing down what the question is that you must answer. Be specific here. Remember our client who was arrested for Driving Under the Influence when observed asleep in a parked car? At the outset, you could formulate an issue such as: Does sleeping in a parked car with the lights and heat on but the engine off constitute driving under the DUI statute? You may revise this, but at the outset, it will help you stay focused on what you need to address.

Draft the discussion section. It may seem strange and out of order to write the discussion before the summary and the facts, however, the discussion section contains your legal analysis. You will need to know what is contained in your analysis before drafting the summary and the facts. Here you will break down the governing rules, identify what needs to be explained, explain the applicable law, and apply it to the client's facts to support your prediction.

Draft the facts. After you have a good idea about what you will say in the discussion, draft the facts section. Why? You won't know what facts will be decisive until you fully understand the legal analysis. Knowing the decisive facts for your case will depend on what the decisive facts were in the cases you will use. Thus, it's better to wait until you know and understand the law before drafting the facts.

Draft the brief answer or summary. This is the last section to write. Because you will have to synthesize the law and facts into a clear and concise summary, it is impossible to get this right before you understand your analysis.

BREAKDOWN OF THE PARTS OF AN INTEROFFICE LEGAL MEMORANDUM

As discussed above, although you will not write the parts of the memorandum in this order, we have described each in the order they would appear in the document.

The Heading

The purpose of a heading in a legal memorandum (or "legal memo") is self-evident: it identifies the recipient, author, and date. The reference (Re:) line should identify the client file (sometimes by a number) and the specific issue being addressed. The best practice is to be as specific as possible. Inter-office memoranda become a part of a client's file and can be resources for later research or preparation for a deposition, client meeting, trial, or appeal. Office memoranda might also be used by lawyers who are researching the same issue but for a different client. Thus, being clear in the reference (Re:) line is essential. If this line only contained "Clover Legal Question," a later reader would have to search the document to find out the specific issue. How you label documents is of critical importance. This is also true for how you save memoranda in a computer file. You want to be able to easily access the memorandum not just by client name but also by subject matter.

EXAMPLE A: Correct heading

To: Sally Lawyer
From: Lester Associate
Date: September 10, 20XX
Re: Robert Reno; # 55-211167; Contract—2010 Employment
        Contract-Enforceability of Non-Compete Clause

EXAMPLE B: Incorrect heading

To: Sally Lawyer
From: Lester Associate
Date: September 10, 2013
Re: Robert Reno file

Notice that the specificity of **Example A** makes it more easily identifiable and enduring.

The Issue or Question Presented

The terms "issue" and "question presented" are interchangeable in a legal memorandum. Typically, this is a matter of personal stylistic preference. This part of the memorandum identifies the exact question you have been asked to analyze. The form of the question will vary depending on the type of analysis you are doing.

For example, where the question relates only to a specific law, absent a client's particular facts, then the issue will only contain the controlling law and specific legal question:

Issue

Under New Hampshire law, what steps are required to initiate and carry out eviction proceedings for a tenant who has not paid rent?

If the issue relates to a particular client's legal problem, then the question presented will contain the controlling law, the specific legal question, and decisive facts:

Under Magnolia Driving Under the Influence (DUI) law, did Mr. Clover "drive" on a way when he was found sleeping in the driver's seat of his car with the accessories in use but the engine off? This matches the above Issue.

Although supervisors may prefer the issue to be written a certain way, when writing an interoffice memorandum on a client's question or problem, the issue should contain the following three parts:

1. The controlling law: Under Magnolia's Driving Under the Influence (DUI) law,
2. The specific legal question: Did Mr. Clover "drive" on a "way" when . . .
3. The Key facts that orient the reader to the context for the question: . . . when he was found sleeping in the driver's seat of his car with the accessories in use but the engine off?

Notice the format and connecting words in bold:

Under Magnolia's Driving Under the Influence (DUI) law, **did** Mr. Clover "drive" on a "way" **when** he was found sleeping in the driver's seat of his car...?

Using the under/did/when format allows you to include all three parts in one sentence. At times the facts will be too lengthy to include in one sentence. For example:

EXAMPLE: A longer issue containing several sentences

Susan Stanford went into shock while witnessing her son go into cardiac arrest as he recovered from routine hernia surgery. Hospital personnel had to revive Stanford's son after an anesthesia pump alarm accidentally failed, giving him an

---

overdose of intravenous morphine. <u>Does Lilyview Hospital have a duty to Stanford for emotional distress injuries resulting from this incident under Connecticut law?</u>

The longer issue also includes all three components: controlling law, the specific legal question, and the client's decisive facts. When writing an issue, here are some things to consider:

- Do not include excess information that distracts or obscures the point.

EXAMPLE: An issue with too much information

Daniel Stanford, an 18-year-old, underwent routine hernia surgery at Lilyview Hospital on February 2, 20XX. As he was recovering, he was hooked up to a morphine pump to control pain. His mother, Susan Stanford, sat by his bed and witnessed her son's lips turn blue and his breathing stop as a loud beeping came from the pump. Stanford now experiences headaches and insomnia from the shock of the incident. Is Lilyview liable to Stanford for these injuries under Connecticut law?

These facts will appear in other sections of your memo. In your Issue, you want to provide the decisive facts, the facts that give rise to the question.

- Avoid being too general or skimping on decisive facts in an issue. Your goal is to identify the *precise* combined factual and legal question that you are analyzing.

EXAMPLES: Issues that are too general

What constitutes "texting" under the statute prohibiting "Texting While Walking"?

Is Lilyview Hospital liable to Susan Stanford for negligent infliction of emotional distress?

Here, we do not know what the controlling jurisdiction is or any client facts that gave rise to the question.

Here, we also do not know the controlling jurisdiction or the facts that could make the hospital liable.

PRACTICAL TIP

Write a draft of your issue before you begin your research. Revise the issue after your research is complete. Revise it again after you finish writing the whole discussion section. You want to begin with a question that orients you to the issue at hand so that you do not go off on a tangent. As you become more of an expert in the particular legal question you are analyzing, you can better draft a specific and effective issue.

The Brief Answer or Summary

The brief answer or summary answers the issue and briefly justifies the answer. The purpose is to tell the reader up-front what the memorandum is about. A busy legal reader (and most legal readers are busy) may only look at the summary of the memorandum at first to get a quick idea of where the case is going. The summary should be precise, clear, and short.

> **PRACTICAL TIP**
>
> Once you work in a legal office, ask to see some sample interoffice legal memoranda. These will give you an idea of what the office's conventions are regarding style and format. You can find out what type of issues (or questions presented) and summaries (or brief answers) the office uses.

The components of an effective summary or brief answer are:

- A quick answer. This can be "yes" or "no." Or, if your conclusion is less certain, the quick answer can reflect that. It is acceptable to say "probably yes" or "likely yes" or "probably no."
- A summary of the rule or rules upon which your conclusion is grounded.
- A short application of the facts to the legal rule or rules.
- An alert to the reader of issues or sub-elements not being addressed.

In practice, a summary does not include any citations even if it refers to law from cases and statutes. Being concise and making the information easily accessible is never more important than in the summary. However, because this goes against general plagiarism concerns, check with your professor or supervisor to be certain this approach is acceptable.

EXAMPLE: An ineffective summary

New Hampshire's test for duty turns on whether a victim contemporaneously perceives the negligent act. To determine if a defendant is liable the plaintiff must prove that: a) the injury was foreseeable; b) the defendant was at fault; c) the accident caused the injury; and d) expert testimony exists that proves plaintiff's physical symptoms. Lilyview Hospital was liable to Susan Stanford because she witnessed her son's cardiac arrest after his hernia surgery.

No specific answer given

Legal rule does not address specific issue of plaintiff's contemporaneous perception. No clear application of client's facts.

EXAMPLE: Edited to improve effectiveness

Likely yes. Lilyview Hospital likely had a duty to Susan Stanford because her injuries were foreseeable and should have been prevented. The evidence is sufficient to prove the three elements of New Hampshire's foreseeability test for duty because: (1) Sanford was the mother of the initial victim, (2) she was close in proximity to the victim at the time of the accident, and (3) she contemporaneously perceived the accident when she heard the loud beep and saw her son in cardiac arrest. Since the hospital has conceded its breach caused Stanford's injury, only the duty question will be answered here.

Quick answer

Rule together with a brief application of client facts

Alert of what is not addressed

The Facts

The facts section explains the background and decisive facts that led to the legal problem. For an interoffice memorandum, the facts can be from client or witness interviews, depositions, transcripts, police reports, or any other documents that form the basis of the legal problem. This section contains no legal analysis. It can be organized chronologically or by topic if there is more than one issue in the case. The facts should read like a story, pulling the reader through the narrative of what happened in an easily readable format. If the facts are complex, subheadings help create a reader-friendly document.

PRACTICAL TIP

As with the issue, it is a good idea to write a draft of the facts first and then redraft when you have completed your legal analysis. Write and revise the facts section last.

It may seem odd to draft the facts section after you have a draft of the issue, summary, and discussion sections. The logic of using this order is that you won't know which facts matter until you have a true grasp of the legal analysis. Once you understand the law you will know which are the critical facts of your client's case—the ones that, if they were slightly different, could affect the outcome. For example, in the case involving the client accused of texting while walking, we know that what she was doing on her phone (looking at directions) is critical to the outcome of her case. The facts section of a memorandum about the texting client must include that detail.

Thus, the first step involves identifying the critical facts. The next step is to identify the background facts that give context to the case. In the Clover case, for example, it may not be a critical fact that he went to a party, but it helps to give the reader a picture of the event. Knowing why he was drinking gives context to facts. Think about how you can paint a vivid picture of what happened. Once you have a list of background facts, make an outline that organizes the facts chronologically or by some other logic. Remember that you want your reader to get a good sense of the players in your case.

Any adverse facts must be included. Your analysis will address the adverse facts, most likely in your counter-analysis (see Chapter 11). Don't be afraid to acknowledge these.

Include procedural facts if the reader needs them to give context to the case. You can also include what the task at hand is in the case. Here is an example of procedural facts and the task from the sample memorandum on page 77:

The State charged Mr. Clover with Driving Under the Influence and now seeks our advice as to whether the State can prove its case against him.

Here are the steps to take in drafting the facts section:

1. Make a list of the critical facts.
2. Identify the background facts.
3. Outline the order in which you will describe the facts.
4. Draft the facts.
5. Cross-check the facts in your discussion section to ensure you have mentioned every critical fact. Do not refer to a fact in the discussion section without putting it in the facts section.
6. If your facts are long (more than three pages), consider using subheadings.
7. Make sure that your facts tell a story. The facts should not sound like a list.
8. Revise.

PRACTICAL TIP

You may need to give citation references to the facts in a legal memo. This will depend on the type of memo you are drafting and a law office's customary practice. Sometimes office memos include a cite after every sentence in the facts. For example, this section could include facts from a deposition or a police report. Ask to see sample memos or ask whether the facts should include citations. *ALWD* and the *Bluebook* include instructions for how to cite documents.

The Discussion Section

The discussion section of the memorandum contains the legal analysis. This is where the law guiding your answer is explained and applied to your client's facts. If this were a math problem, this would be where you "show your work." The discussion section serves to justify the conclusion or prediction you are making about the likely outcome of the case.

Perhaps more than any other part of the legal memorandum, the discussion section usually follows a set structure; specifically, explain the law before you apply it to the client's facts in the discussion section. Look back at the example interoffice memorandum on Mr. Clover's driving question on page 78. Notice that the discussion section starts with a paragraph stating the relevant rules. The memo then has paragraphs that explain the law, followed by paragraphs that apply the law.

The discussion section is the most complex part and the heart of the memorandum, which is why Chapter 9 is devoted entirely to this section of the memorandum.

The Conclusion

The conclusion section of a legal memo typically reiterates your overall "answer" to the client's problem. Thus, it should concisely summarize how you think the case will turn out. Note that you do not always need to include a conclusion section. It depends on your style and the demands of the reader for whom you are writing. Usually, this section sums up the analysis and is almost a mirror of the brief answer.

Writing the Discussion Section of an Interoffice Memorandum

INTRODUCTION

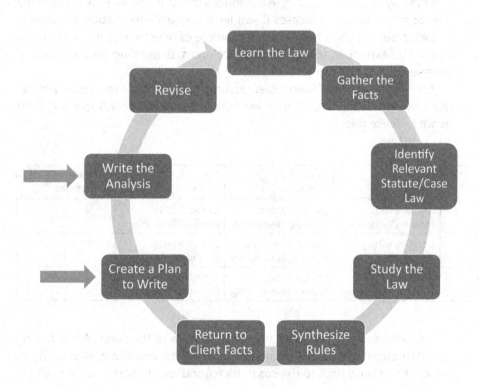

Writing the discussion section of a memorandum is a multistep process. We already identified the legal issue and the relevant law, studied the law, synthesized the rule, and returned to the client's facts to find the decisive facts. In this chapter, we discuss how to organize the information within a discussion section. One guiding organizational principle is that lawyers explain the law before they apply it.

Now, we can begin the writing process:

1. *Make an outline of your legal analysis.* Every legal analysis should begin with an outline so you know how the pieces of the analysis fit together and how you will structure the analysis on the page. One suggestion for an outline format will be made here, but you will eventually develop a style of outlining that works for you.
2. *Write a draft of the analysis.* This is where you will use some version of the CREAC structure discussed in Chapter 6.
3. *Revise the draft.*
4. *Revise the draft again as needed.*
5. *Proofread and line edit.*

HOW TO ORGANIZE THE INFORMATION

One way to organize multiple authorities is to use a chart. It can help to see the commonalities in the cases if you lay out visually the important aspects of each case. The chart below is one example of how to organize authorities. It could be expanded to include other columns, depending on the case and your personal preferences.

For example, in Mr. Clover's case, assume that you must research each element of DUI: (1) driving, (2) on a way, (3) while under the influence. A chart might look like this:

Element	Winstead	O' Malley	Holloran	Synthesized Rule on Element
"Driving"	Decisive facts: Holding/Reasoning:	Decisive facts: Holding/Reasoning:	Decisive facts: Holding/Reasoning:	
"On a way"	Decisive facts: Holding/Reasoning:	Decisive facts: Holding/Reasoning:	Decisive facts: Holding/Reasoning:	
"Under the influence"	Decisive facts: Holding/Reasoning:	Decisive facts: Holding/Reasoning:	Decisive facts: Holding/Reasoning:	

You also want to develop a way to keep track of the cases. Avoid having to leaf through each case to remind yourself what it was about. Although you will continually go back to the cases, it's a good idea to have a form to use to brief each case.

Make an Outline[1]

Often students arrive in law school unaccustomed to making an outline. In legal writing, this step is critical because it forces you to think through the concepts clearly before you put pen to paper to start writing a draft. The outlining process begins during your research. You can tinker with the outline as your research progresses. Outlining will move you from analysis to writing.

When you start outlining, you will probably be lost in a welter of concepts, facts, law, and reasoning. When you complete your outline, you will understand the analysis and have a logical, linear roadmap that directs you through the issues, sub-issues, rules, cases, facts, and counterarguments to the conclusion. Then you can write efficiently.

One caveat here: for some, writing an outline is not how to begin the process.[2] You may need to get words on a page first, which Anne Lamott calls the "down draft."[3] If you fit that description, try making a skeletal outline first, so you have some idea of where you are going, then go ahead and write. *But* after you finish the "down draft," you'll need to organize what you wrote. You may find that after you have downloaded your ideas on paper, you can better see and understand a clear structure. The danger in this method arises if, after finishing the down draft, you think you are done. This is very unlikely to be the case. Think of this stage as prewriting, or a "brain dump," followed by putting the text in logical order.

Outlining serves several purposes.

- Outlining puts ideas into linear structure.
- Outlining shows relationships between ideas; for example, which are the overarching and subordinate points.
- Outlining helps you figure out where ideas belong logically.
- Outlining enables you to remember an analysis's different points and nuances.
- Outlining can show you what you understand and where you need more thought and/or research.
- If you do not understand a discussion/argument well enough to outline it, you do not understand it well enough to write it.
- If you do not outline, you are guaranteed to waste time reorganizing and rewriting. In addition, you will probably forget to include important details.

---

1. The information on outlining derives from materials by Alice Briggs, the former Writing Specialist at UNH Law.
2. See Robbins, Johansen, and Chestek, *Your Client's Story*, p. 116.
3. See Anne Lamott, *Bird by Bird*, p. 25.

Format

- There is no "winning" formula for how you format an outline. It is entirely personal and should work for you.
- At a minimum, the format must distinguish between overarching points and subordinate points. Frequently ordinals (I, A, 1, a, etc.) show these points. In other words, using bullets that simply list the points will probably not be helpful.

Process

- Every writer develops a personal process for outlining. There is no one right way, provided the final outline is complete and useful and the process for getting there is efficient.
- Do not be afraid to make several outlines. This can help you learn the analysis and enable you to explore different organizations to see which works best.
- Outlining can be done in phases or iterations, as discussed below, as your understanding of the analysis develops.
- Some writers begin with all the points they want to make and organize (bottom-up outlining); others begin with the major points they want to make and then add the details (top-down outlining). Many writers use a combination of these approaches.

STEP-BY-STEP APPROACH TO MAKING AN OUTLINE

Step 1. Identify the major steps or ideas in the analysis.

- Frequently, this will mean identifying the rule and its elements or factors.
- For example, if the topic is, "When is a prior incident admissible in a defendant's criminal trial?" the rule would have three elements: (1) the evidence must be relevant for a purpose other than showing the defendant's character, (2) there must be clear proof that the defendant committed the act, and (3) the probative value must outweigh the prejudicial impact.
- You figure out the elements of a rule by looking at how the courts approach the rule. What topics do the courts discuss? What conclusions does a court draw in reaching its holding?
- You must synthesize cases and put together a rule incorporating new aspects to the rule that the court added. Remember Cases A, B, and C on page 67. Case C added an aspect to the rule (communication with another does not have to be live), and this should be included in the rule.

Step 2. Begin with a roadmap/global section.

- This is where you put all the information that the reader needs to understand the rest of the discussion/analysis.
  - If a piece of information is relevant to just one element, then it probably does not belong in the roadmap section.
  - If a piece of information is relevant to the entire discussion/analysis, it belongs in the roadmap section.
- Things to consider putting in the roadmap section include:
  - The answer to the question you've been asked.
  - The roadmap or overall rule.
  - Any interpretive standards that courts use when applying the rule. For example, do courts interpret the rule broadly or narrowly? Do courts apply the rule frequently or infrequently?
  - Any policy or purpose behind the rule.
  - Who carries the burden.
  - The relationships between elements or factors in the rule.
  - Any "givens"; that is, things that are already established or that you are not going to discuss.

Step 3. Make a section for each major step/idea/element.

- You may find as you proceed that you can combine two elements into one section but separating them into separate sections is a good way to begin.
- Ask yourself whether each major idea/element needs to be broken down into sub-elements.
  - For example, the relevance element of the New Hampshire rule on admissibility of a prior incident can be broken down into subparts, direct bearing on an issue actually in dispute, and a clear and logical connection between the prior act and the current charge. The clear and logical connection also breaks into two subparts (prior incident is factually similar and close in time).

Step 4. Put the sections into a logical sequence.

- To determine the logical sequence, first decide whether the courts typically employ a certain sequence.
- If the courts do not use a particular sequence, then ask yourself whether logic compels a certain sequence. For example, does one element depend on another? In this case the dependent element must come after the primary element.
- If neither the courts nor logic dictates a sequence, start with the strongest element or the element that is most important to the client; put

the second strongest/most important element last; and put any other elements in between in descending order of importance.

Step 5. Write out the rules.

- Here you want to draft the rules and subrules.

Step 6. Indicate which case(s) you will use to illustrate/support/prove each point you need to make about the rule.

- Generally using more than one case is preferable.
- Consider using cases that show different aspects or parameters of the rule.
- Provide some citation information. These do not need to be full *Bluebook* cites; a case name and a pincite, or even just a case name is sufficient. Including cites keeps you from making up propositions that you can't support. It is also a useful tool when you are writing from the outline.

> **NOTE**
>
> The next steps require going back to flesh out the outline and should be done for each section and subsection of the outline. You may choose to complete one section before beginning another, or you may decide to put rules in all the sections before moving to the next step.

Step 7. Identify which case(s) you are going to analogize to/distinguish from the client's facts.

Step 8. Make a list of all the points that might be relevant to this discussion/argument that you have not included in the outline.

- These may be points about the law or about the facts.
- Think about each point in the context of the outline and insert it where it makes logical sense.

Step 9. Write a conclusion for each section.

- You may change this conclusion as your analysis develops.

Step 10. Check for completeness.

- At this point, stop and consider whether the rule and the cases supporting it will support all the points/arguments you want to make about your client's facts.

- If you want to make a point/argument but the rule explanation doesn't support it, then you need to expand the rule explanation.

EXAMPLE: Outline of Albert Memorandum Discussion Section: Roadmap Paragraph and Relevance

I. Roadmap: Prior Act Evidence Admissibility
   A. Evidence is likely admissible because A:
      1. Claims accident
      2. 2 acts (ham/turkey) are similar
      3. Witnesses offer clear proof A. acted
      4. High probative value/low prejudicial value
   B. Rule 404(b) allows prior act evidence if:
      1. Relevant for purpose other than D's character
      2. Clear proof exists D committed acts
      3. Probative value outweighs possible prejudice to D
   C. State has burden. *McGlew* @ 1193.
   D. 404(b) purpose is trial on merits, not character. *Bassett* @ 893.
II. Relevance: Direct Bearing on Issue in Dispute Explained
   A. Turkey incident is relevant
   B. Evidence relevant if it has direct bearing on issue in dispute.
   C. *McGlew* @ 1194.
      1. Evidence has a direct bearing if to show absence of accident
         a. *Lesnick* admits prior act b/c D (wife) claimed stabbing of husband was accident in charged crime and prior act. @ 690.
         b. *Blackey* excludes evidence because D did not claim accident. @ 1334.
III. Relevance: Direct Bearing on Issue in Dispute Applied to Albert's case
      2. Turkey has a direct bearing on whether Albert shoplifted.
         a. As *Lesnick* wife claimed 2 stabbings accidental, A claims both meat incidents accidental.
         b. Unlike *Blackey* D, A has claimed accident.
         c. (conclusion) Ct will find A's claim of accident puts her intent at issue by claiming accident.
IV. Relevance: Clear and Logical Connection Explained
      3. Clear logical connection where factually similar, close in time
         a. Precise chain of reasoning must be articulated.
            i. *Lesnick* same weapon, victim, circumstances and few months apart, so prosecution could "articulate precise chain of reasoning" @ 690.

---

b. Acts must be factually similar.
  i. *McGlew* no connection because different victim age, gender, and 6 years span between incidents, so not "clear and logical" that intent was the same @ 1194.
V. Clear and Logical Connection: Applied to Albert's Case
  4. Turkey has a clear and logical connection to the charged crime
    a. Same type of product, similar removal from store, close in time; compare *Lesnick*.
    b. Unlike *McGlew* where State could not articulate precise chain of reasoning because facts too different.
    c. (conclusion) Ct. likely find "clear and logical" connection because of similarities.
VI. Turkey Incident Meets 404(b) Relevance Requirement

EXPLAINING THE LAW IN A DISCUSSION

Remember, in legal writing, we use structure. When you are writing a legal analysis of an issue, first, you give the explanation of the law, followed by the application of the law to your client's facts. The structure may vary depending on your client's problem and your audience, but generally, you always explain the law before you apply it.

Explaining the law to the reader requires first beginning with the overall synthesized rule. Next, you explain more specifically how the rule works. If the rule is based on a statute, then the explanation may focus on further defining terms or construction. To do this, you may have to explain cases where the court defines and applies the term to specific situations. Our analysis of whether Mr. Clover was "driving" provides an example of this.

If there is no statute that applies to the client's problem, the issue you are addressing may only involve explaining a rule that is based on common law cases. Or you may be dealing with a statute where further explanation really isn't necessary. For example, in Mr. Clover's case, we could be asked to find the law on what the legal limits are on blood alcohol in New Hampshire. There is a clear-cut answer to this, and thus no analysis would be necessary.

The challenge of writing about the law is that you will need to take what can be complex concepts and explain them in simple, understandable language. Whether you are explaining the law to a client, a colleague, or a judge, you must always use plain English and strive for simple, accurate descriptions of the law.

Think about the steps we have already taken in our sample case file that have laid the groundwork for our discussion or analysis. We have studied the statute and cases, briefed the cases, synthesized the rule, and outlined the analysis.

In this chapter, you will learn an approach to explaining the law. On page 104, you will learn how to apply the specific law to your client's case.

The Roadmap (aka Global) Paragraph

At the beginning of a legal discussion, you give the reader an overall roadmap of the analysis that is to come. Other terms for describing this paragraph are the "global paragraph" or the "rule(s) paragraph." Here, we will refer to it as the roadmap paragraph. If readers only have a few minutes and want to quickly understand your conclusion on the issue, they can do so just by reading your roadmap paragraph. Once readers have more time, they can come back and read the remainder of the discussion.

Remember, in legal writing, conclusions come first. A roadmap paragraph should begin with your overall conclusion about the case, giving your reader the prediction you are making. This is followed by the overall rule. The overall rule comes from a statute, case law, or both. The overall rule may be a synthesized rule that you have distilled from multiple cases. Next, you include policy *if* it is relevant to your prediction. Finally, the roadmap paragraph alerts the reader if there are issues that you are not going to address.

In the following example, the issue is the enforceability of a noncompete clause in a client's contract in Nebraska. A noncompete clause is a common part of an employment contract that restricts an employee from leaving employment and immediately using assets like goodwill, training, trade secrets, or client lists to compete against the employer.

EXAMPLE: A roadmap paragraph where the overall rule comes from case law and includes policy.

DISCUSSION

The noncompete clause in Lyle Lovell's contract is likely not enforceable because it covered more geographic territory than reasonably necessary to protect Sunshine's legitimate business interest in its driver education company. Typically, a noncompete clause is only enforceable when it is (1) not greater than is reasonably necessary to protect the employer in some legitimate interest, (2) not unduly harsh and oppressive on the employee, and (3) reasonable in the sense that it is not injurious to the

Overall conclusion

Overall rule based on common law

---

public. *Mertz v. Pharmacists Mut. Ins. Co.*, 625 N.W.2d 197, 204
(Neb. 2001). Failure to meet any of the three elements is grounds
to invalidate the provision and reformation of unreasonable
provisions is not allowed. *Vlasin v. Len Johnson & Co., Inc.*, 455
N.W.2d 772, 776 (Neb. 1990). This test promotes a reasonable
balance between the employer's interests, the employee's

Policy   prospects, and the public good. *See Dow v. Gotch*, 201 N.W. 655,
657 (Neb. 1924); *Am. Sec. Ser., Inc. v. Vodra*, 385 N.W.2d 73, 80
(Neb. 1986).

The next excerpt is from the sample memorandum on page 8.

**EXAMPLE: A roadmap paragraph where the overall rule is based
on case law, and policy is not included.**

DISCUSSION

Overall conclusion

Overall rule from case law

    Albert's prior act involving the turkey is relevant for a purpose
other than character because she raised the issue of intent, and
the prior act is factually similar and close in time to the charged
act. Evidence is relevant for a purpose other than character if it
(1) has a direct bearing on an issue actually in dispute, and (2) a
clear and logical connection exists between that act and the crime
charged. *McGlew*, 658 A.2d at 1194. The trial court must make
specific findings on each of these elements. *Id.*

Here the issue is whether the client, who was having car trouble, "tres-
passed" when she entered a home after knocking. The homeowner had not
heard the knocking and was surprised by the client inside the house.

**EXAMPLE: A roadmap paragraph where the overall rule is based
on a statute and case law.**

Overall conclusion

Statutory rule

    Our client, Ms. Carter, likely did not know that she was neither
licensed nor privileged to enter Mr. Hall's residence, and thus a
conviction against her for trespass is unlikely. Vermont's criminal trespass statute, based on the Model Penal Code, forbids an
actor from enter[ing] a dwelling house, whether or not a person is
actually present, knowing that the actor is not licensed or privileged to do so. 13 V.S.A. § 3705(d) (2006). *See also* Model Penal

Code §221.2(1) (1962). The knowledge requirement establishes a subjective standard; it is insufficient for the state to show that the defendant should have known the entrant was not licensed or privileged to enter the dwelling. *State v. Fanger*, 164 Vt. 48, 52, 665 A.2d 36, 38 (Vt. 1995).

Further statement of overall rule based on case

EXAMPLE FROM SAMPLE CASE FILE: A roadmap paragraph where the overall rule is based on a statute and case law, and includes policy.

Mr. Clover was likely driving a vehicle under Magnolia's DUI statute because he was seated in the driver's seat with the key fob in his pocket, the car lights and heat turned on, prepared to drive. A person violates the Magnolia DUI statute if they "drive or attempt to drive a vehicle upon any way" while they are under the influence of drugs or alcohol. M.G. Rev. Stat. Ann. § 265-A:2 (2022). To meet the statute, three elements must be proved: (1) driving or attempting to drive; (2) on a way; and (3) under the influence. § 265-A:2. As Mr. Clover does not contest that he was under the influence, and another Associate is addressing whether he was on a "way," this memo will focus only whether he was "driving." Driving is defined as operation or being in "actual physical control" of the vehicle. *State v. Holloran*, 669 A.2d 800, 801 (M.G. 1995). The state can prove "actual physical control" if there is circumstantial evidence that the defendant had "the capacity bodily to guide or exercise dominion over the vehicle at the present time" before falling asleep, or that the defendant would "imminent[ly] operate" the vehicle. *State v. Winstead*, 836 A.2d 775, 778 (M.G. 2003); see also *Holloran*, 669 A.2d at 801-02. *But see State v. O'Malley*, 416 A.2d 1387, 1388 (M.G. 2002). "Actual physical control" differentiates between one using a vehicle as a shelter, and one who presents a public safety risk by exercising control of the vehicle while inebriated. *Holloran*, 669 A.2d at 801.

Overall conclusion

Statutory rule

Dispense with elements not discussed

Narrow to relevant rule

Indicate the synthesized parts of the rule that you will explain further from the case law and policy.

Explaining the Law Using Case Examples

Once you have done an outline and constructed the roadmap paragraph in which you give the overall rule that will answer the client's problem, in the following paragraphs, you will break down the rule and show the reader how you arrived at your conclusions about the client's case. Each paragraph explaining the law should begin with the principle or focused point you will explain. Paragraphs in legal writing are like division problems. The answer to the particular problem is at the top of the equation. The contents of the paragraph are where you "show your work" to justify for the reader that your conclusion is right.

How you "show your work" will depend on the type of problem. Typically, the explanation of the law entails using cases to show by example how the court applied each relevant piece of the rule to different factual settings that resemble the facts of your case. Case examples help to both analogize your client's facts and distinguish your client's facts. Remember, our system of law depends on *stare decisis*. Correctly predicting or advocating for a particular result depends on what courts have done in the past, thus, comparing past cases to your client's case shows an accurate and thorough analysis of the law.

Each paragraph should start with the conclusion being supported or explained. Sometimes it will take more than one paragraph to explain a conclusion. In this case, use a clear transition at the start of the paragraph to alert the reader that you continue to support the same conclusion. Using words like "similarly," "likewise," or "on the other hand" tells the reader that you are still explaining the same conclusion as in the preceding paragraph.

A Step-by-Step Approach to Writing the Explanation of the Law

Step 1: Start with a sentence or two stating the principle or focused point.

State the point or the legal principle that the case explanation clarifies and proves to be true. We call these sentences "hooks" or "conclusion" sentences. This sentence specifies and explicitly connects the reader to the part of the overall rule in the roadmap paragraph that you are addressing. You will learn more specifically how to write these sentences later in this Chapter. Use the present tense when stating the focus sentence or legal principle. Notice in the example below that the first conclusion sentence uses the same term "legitimate business interest" to alert the reader that this is the term that will be defined in the paragraph. The first sentence of the next paragraph further breaks down the meaning of "legitimate business interest" and draws the reader's attention to the definition of "unfair competition."

DISCUSSION

The noncompete clause in Lyle Lovell's contract is likely unenforceable because it covers more geographic territory than reasonably necessary to protect Sunshine's legitimate business interest in its driver education company. Typically, courts enforce a noncompete clause when it is (1) not greater than is reasonably necessary to protect the employer in some legitimate interest, (2) not unduly harsh and oppressive on the employee, and (3) reasonable in the sense that it is not injurious to the public. *Mertz v. Pharmacists Mut. Ins. Co.*, 625 N.W.2d 197, 204 (Neb. 2001). Failure to meet any of the three elements can invalidate the provision and reformation of unreasonable provisions is not allowed. *Vlasin v. Len Johnson & Co., Inc.*, 455 N.W.2d 772, 776 (Neb. 1990). This test promotes a reasonable balance between the employer's interests, the employee's prospects, and the public good. *See Dow v. Gotch*, 201 N.W. 655, 657 (Neb. 1924); *Am. Sec. Ser., Inc. v. Vodra*, 385 N.W.2d 73, 80 (Neb. 1986).

Overall conclusion

Overall rule based on common law

Policy

An employer has a legitimate business interest in protection against improper and unfair competition, but not against use of general skills or knowledge obtainable from a similar business. *Moore*, 562 N.W.2d at 540; *Boisen*, 383 N.W.2d at 34. *Polly v. Ray D. Hilderman & Co.*, 407 N.W.2d 751, 755 (Neb. 1987) Unfair competition is distinguished from ordinary competition by evaluating an employee's opportunity to appropriate goodwill from the employer. *Boisen*, 383 N.W.2d at 33. For example, in *Polly*, where an accountant had substantial personal contact with approximately forty-six of his employer's accounts, the court found that the accounting firm had a legitimate interest in protecting itself against the accountant's opportunity to appropriate customer goodwill after his employment was terminated. 407 N.W. 2d at 756.

Rule statement that focuses on one part of the overall rule—definition of legitimate business interest. Next, writer defines unfair competition. Finally, writer shows an example of how a court has applied the term "unfair competition."

Step 2: Construct your case description.

Before you write about the cases that serve as examples of how the court applies the legal principles you base your prediction on, you need to have done the necessary background thinking. To write an effective case description, you need to have first studied and distilled what the key cases hold. This means you must:

- Identify the court's holding (or the court's answer to the relevant legal question before it).

- Identify the court's reasoning (why the court decided the relevant legal question the way it did).
- Identify critical/legally significant facts in the case.
- Identify the legal principle that the case illustrates (the "focus sentence").

Step 3: Write the case description.

Include only critical/legally significant facts and any context facts necessary for the reader to understand the case: reasoning and holding.

Step 4: Do's and don'ts.

- DO use the past tense when describing a case.
- DO NOT use party names, instead use party designations. For example, instead of using Mr. Winstead (from the sample case file: Winstead case), use "defendant." Other designations can include "plaintiff" or descriptors such as "patron," "driver," or "employer." Designating the parties by the roles they play in the case makes it easier for your reader to understand the legal principles addressed in the case.

EXAMPLES:

NOT HELPFUL: Here, the writer uses names, making it difficult to discern the significance of the parties' roles.

For example, in *Polly*, where Mr. Polly had substantial personal contact with approximately forty-six of Hilderman's accounts, the court found that Hilderman had a legitimate interest in protecting itself against Polly's opportunity to appropriate customer goodwill after his employment was terminated. 407 N.W.2d at 756.

HELPFUL: Here, the writer uses designations. Notice that significance of the parties' actions are easier to discern "unfair competition."

For example, in *Polly*, where an accountant had substantial personal contact with approximately forty-six of his employer's accounts, the court found that the accounting firm had a legitimate interest in protecting itself against the accountant's opportunity to appropriate customer goodwill after his employment was terminated. 407 N.W.2d at 756.

- Give the reader only necessary information. Do not include procedural information unless it is critical to the issue. Do not include background facts other than to give the description necessary context.

EXAMPLES:

For example, in *Polly*, the plaintiff appealed a wage collection decision of the district court sustaining the plaintiff's motion for summary judgment and the court affirmed the district court's decision. 407 N.W.2d at 753. The court found that the accounting firm had a legitimate interest in protecting itself against the accountant's opportunity to appropriate customer goodwill after his employment was terminated. *Id.* at 756. The ruling was based on the accountant having had substantial personal contact with approximately 46 of his employer's accounts. *Id.*

> NOT HELPFUL: The procedural information here is not decisively relevant to the key issue—the enforceability of the noncompete clause.

In *Holloran*, on March 15, 1994, police found the inebriated defendant asleep in Londonderry, New Hampshire, in the driver's seat of his pickup truck with the keys in the ignition; he was awaiting a phone call from his wife to pick her up from a Tupperware party. *Id.* at 800.

> NOT HELPFUL: Reader does not need to know the date or the exact place where the incident occurred.

- When using more than one case to illustrate the legal principle, be sure to connect the cases, making it clear to the reader why the cases are being addressed within the same paragraph (or paragraphs) to prove a principle. Using words like "similarly," "likewise," or "in contrast" will alert your reader about how the cases should be read together.
- Avoid writing a report of cases. Remember that the reader needs more than just what each case said. The reader needs to understand the principle and the cases help exemplify those principles. If each paragraph begins with "In [case name]" the reader has no context for why the case is relevant.

Evidence of a prior act is relevant to refute a defendant's claim that the crime was committed by accident. *Lesnick*, 677 A.2d at 690. For example, the court in *Lesnick* admitted evidence of a prior act because it was relevant to show the absence of an accident where the defendant claimed she had stabbed her husband in self-defense because she believed him to be an unknown intruder. *Id.* In contrast, where the defendant denied any involvement at all in the crime, the court excluded the evidence. *State v. Blackey*, 623 A.2d 1331, 1332-33 (N.H. 1993). The evidence was not relevant because, by denying the crime altogether, the defendant had not placed her intent at issue. *Id.*

> HELPFUL: Sentence that identifies the legal principle described in the paragraph below.
>
> Court's holding
>
> Court's reasoning

EXAMPLE: SAMPLE FROM CASE FILE

To prove actual physical control, the driver must have the capacity bodily to guide or exercise control over the vehicle. *Winstead,* 836 A.2d at 778. In *Winstead,* the defendant was found asleep and intoxicated upright in the driver's seat of his car, engine running, in a Wal-Mart parking lot. *Id.* at 776. The defendant testified that before falling asleep, he had unlocked the driver's side door, sat down, pressed the clutch, moved the car into neutral, started the engine, and turned on the heater. *Id.* at 778. Given the steps taken, and that starting the car comes "as close as possible" to operation, the court held that the defendant was in actual physical control of his vehicle before falling asleep. *Id.* (citing *Atkinson v. State*, 331 M.G. 199, 201 (M.G. 1993)).

Margin notes:

Starts with sentence that identifies the legal principle to be explained in the paragraph.

Introduction to *Winstead* starting with decisive facts

Court's reasoning and holding

APPLYING THE LAW IN A DISCUSSION

Because our legal system is grounded in *stare decisis,* precedent cases typically support legal analysis. Ultimately, whomever you are writing an analysis for will want assurance that there is ample support for the prediction you are making. The reader will want to see that you are a reliable legal analyst. Judges want to get the law right—they want to exercise their judgment fairly. Although your first internships and summer jobs may not require you to write a persuasive analysis for a judge, your supervisors may use your work to persuade a judge of a particular position on behalf of a client. Your analysis may also demonstrate to a client that a particular position is supported. Here, too, you will need ample precedent to justify your position.

Explaining the law, using specific examples of how courts have applied legal principles to problems similar to the client's, is the first step in an effective legal analysis. The next step is showing the reader *why* the prior cases support your prediction. Writing case comparisons requires explicitness and precision. Readers have no use for broad legal conclusions without specific support. This section will provide you with an approach to writing a case comparison.

Effective case comparisons require that you know your client's facts. You must comb through the client's facts and identify those that matter to an outcome. Similar to the decisive facts cited by the court in an opinion, your client's decisive facts are the ones that decide the issue. Refer to the discussion about background versus decisive facts on page 70. Take away a particular fact, and the outcome changes. You cannot judge the relevant client facts until you know the law. Once you understand the law, you can determine which facts matter by comparing client facts to the critical precedent case facts.

Applying the law to your client's problem builds upon the explanation of the relevant law. The explanation of the law and the application should form a parallel structure. The case examples show how a court applies the rule in other situations, and those examples should match up with the facts you are focusing on in your client's case. Thus, once you explain the law, you begin to construct your comparisons—both the analogies and the distinctions. Keep in mind the legal rule that will be applied, the court's reasoning, and the outcome you are predicting as you proceed through the following steps.

1. Identify critical/legally significant facts in the prior case (i.e., the one you're using to make the analogy). Remember, these are the facts that the court's holding turns on.

2. Identify critical/legally significant facts in your client's case.

3. Identify how the critical facts make your case similar to or different from the prior case. Important note: If you can't make a direct, one-to-one fact comparison, you may still make the analogy or distinction by focusing on a different level of comparison; for example, you cannot compare apples to oranges, but at a more abstract level, both are fruit. The case facts may also be so different that they help prove your point. For example, let's say in Mr. Clover's case there was an opinion, we will call it Case A, where the defendant had gone off the road, turned off the car, and moved to the back seat. Let's say further that the court found that the defendant was not "driving" because these facts proved that he had no intent to drive and that they showed no indication of control over the car. The case could be useful in deciding if Mr. Clover was "driving." Even though the facts are different, you can contrast, or distinguish, Mr. Clover's facts that he was in the driver's seat compared to the driver in Case A, who was in the back seat. Since the court found that being in the back seat demonstrated no intent to drive, Case A might reach the opposite conclusion (intent to drive) in Mr. Clover's situation.

4. Identify the legal significance of the overlapping facts. In other words, use the reasoning that the court applied in the prior decision to predict the outcome when the rule is applied in your client's case.

5. Construct your comparison or distinction:

Start with a sentence in which you state the point the analogy is intended to make.

EXAMPLE A: Sentence that *does not state* the point of the analogy

"Albert's case is similar to the facts of *Lesnick*." This sentence does not tell the reader the substance of why the case comparison matters.

EXAMPLE B: Sentence that *states* the point of the analogy

"Albert's prior act is relevant here because Albert claims she took the ham by accident." This sentence tells the reader why the comparison matters.

6. Write the rest of the analogy. Compare the critical facts in your client's case and the critical facts in the prior case. Make sure to use the appropriate level of detail. Be specific and concrete, but don't include any nonessential facts.

EXAMPLE A: Analogy that lacks sufficient, decisive detail:

"Like the defendant in *Lesnick*, where the prior act was admitted, here Albert's prior act should be similarly admitted." Notice that the writer is comparing broad legal concepts instead of specific significant facts.

EXAMPLE B: Analogy with sufficient, decisive detail:

"Like the defendant in *Lesnick*, who admitted the stabbing but claimed it was an accident, Albert made her intent an issue by claiming she took the ham unintentionally." Notice the explicit detail.

Analogies that lack sufficient depth and detail fail to reliably justify your conclusion on the problem.

Here are some ways to help the reader understand the comparison:

a. Place the facts from the two cases close together.
b. Explicitly make the comparison using words like "like" or "similar to" or "unlike."

c. Use parallel structure.

d. Compare like items.

7. Use "because"! So much of legal analysis requires you to justify why you think a particular outcome is likely. Explain why the comparison matters by applying the reasoning from the prior case to your client's facts. In this way, you inform the reader of the legal significance of the similarity/difference between your client's facts and the facts in the prior case. For example: "Therefore, *because* evidence of the prior act is offered for a purpose other than Albert's character or propensity to steal meat, it is probably admissible."

EXAMPLE: Giving the specific reasoning that supports your prediction.

Covenants that are unduly broad in scope as to time, geography, or activity are void as a matter of public policy, because they hinder competition and free trade. *See Mertz v. Pharmacists Mut. Ins. Co.,* 625 N.W.2d 197, 204 (Neb. 2001). For example, in *Mertz,* a three-year territorial covenant was unenforceable <u>because the covenant summarily precluded all solicitation within the territory rather than being reasonably limited to those customers that he had worked with directly.</u> *Id.* at 204.

The courts are likely to view Reno's noncompete restriction as overly broad and unenforceable. Like the three-year noncompete clause in *Mertz,* that was invalidated because it encompassed customers with whom the employee had never had any contact, Reno's noncompete agreement similarly includes a blanket prohibition that precludes him from soliciting new customers or new markets. <u>The court is likely to invalidate such a clause, as it did in *Mertz,* because it is not narrowly tailored to cover only those customers who Reno had previously contacted.</u>

The underlined portions show the reasoning that supports the prediction.

8. Writing an effective analogy or distinction should help you discover if you have not adequately given decisive facts from a case. The case examples and the analogies and distinctions should focus on the same facts. In other words, the case comparisons in the application of the law should use the facts described in the case explanations. The two sections should include parallel analysis.

EXAMPLE: Explanation of law and application of law—parallel structure with similar use of decisive facts.

Covenants that are unduly broad in scope as to time, geography, or activity are void as a matter of public policy, because they hinder competition and free trade. *See Mertz v. Pharmacists Mut. Ins. Co.*, 625 N.W.2d 197, 204 (Neb. 2001). For example, in *Mertz*, a three-year territorial covenant was unenforceable because the covenant summarily precluded all solicitation within the territory rather than being reasonably limited to those customers that the employee had worked with directly. *Id.* at 204.

The courts are likely to view Reno's noncompete restriction as overly broad and unenforceable. Like the three-year noncompete clause in *Mertz*, that was invalidated because it encompassed customers with whom the employee had never had any contact, Reno's noncompete agreement similarly includes a blanket prohibition that precludes him from soliciting new customers or new markets. The court is likely to invalidate such a clause, as it did in *Mertz*, because it is not narrowly tailored to cover only those customers whom Reno had previously contacted.

The highlighted portions indicate the parallel structure. Notice that each excerpt zeroes in on specific facts.

EXAMPLE: SAMPLE FROM CASE FILE

This is the explanation using the *Winstead* case.

To prove actual physical control, the driver must have the capacity bodily to guide or exercise control over the vehicle. *Winstead*, 836 A.2d at 778. In *Winstead*, the police found the defendant asleep and intoxicated upright in the driver's seat of his car, engine running, in a Wal-Mart parking lot. *Id.* at 776. The defendant testified that before falling asleep, he had unlocked the driver's side door, sat down, pressed the clutch, moved the car into neutral, started the engine, and turned on the heater. *Id.* at 778. Given the steps taken, and that starting the car comes "as close as possible" to operation, the court held that the defendant was in actual physical control of his vehicle before falling asleep. *Id.* (citing *Atkinson v. State*, 331 M.G. 199, 201 (M.G. 1993)).

This is the application paragraph, applying the law from *Winstead* to the facts of Clover's case. Notice the specific facts from *Winstead* and from Clover's case to show the comparison. Notice too the use of *Winstead*'s reasoning (e.g., "as close as possible") to support the conclusion in Clover's case.

Mr. Clover did exercise control over the vehicle because although the engine was not running, he took steps to put his body in a position to drive. Like the defendant in *Winstead* who testified to unlocking his car, pushing in the clutch, shifting to neutral, and turning the engine on to have the heat running,

Mr. Clover fell asleep in the seated position, lights and heat running. Mr. Clover unlocked and entered his car with his key fob nearby, pushed the ignition button and turned on the heat. Even though igniting the engine would take the extra step of pushing in the brake, Mr. Clover, like the defendant in *Winstead*, came as close to operation of the vehicle as possible by seating himself in the ready position and igniting the accessories with the key fob before he fell asleep. Thus, Mr. Clover exercised control over the car and as a result was in actual physical control of the vehicle.

ORGANIZATION: INTERNAL PARAGRAPH STRUCTURE

At this point, we have discussed parts of your analysis. In our sample case file, we studied the law, completed an outline, and written a case illustration and a case comparison. As you move into drafting the complete analysis, pay attention to how the structure hangs together. You want your reader to move easily through the analysis, going from paragraph to paragraph without being interrupted by a point or sentence that does not flow from the roadmap you have provided in the first paragraphs of the discussion section.

Legal analysis must be tightly constructed. The structure begins with the overall paragraph or roadmap. The paragraphs that follow flesh out the legal principles identified in the roadmap paragraph. Each of these paragraphs must be constructed carefully using language that alerts your reader to the point you are supporting. At its most basic level, your writing has an emotional impact on your reader. You hope for a reaction of ease and confidence, not frustration and confusion.

To ensure good structure, first draft the outline (above). This will serve as a guide to keep your overall structure on target. The outline instructs you about the order in which your points must proceed. Once you begin to draft your analysis, follow these rules when writing your paragraphs:

1. Only address one point per paragraph.
2. Keep the paragraphs that explain the law and give examples from the cases separate from paragraphs that apply the law to your client's fact.
3. Begin each paragraph with a clear conclusion that tells the reader the point of the paragraph or with an obvious transition word that signals to the reader that the paragraph is substantively connected to the one preceding.
4. Keep the paragraphs short—no more than one-half a page, but preferably less.

Writing the Paragraph's First Sentence

The point of every paragraph should appear in the first sentence. This sentence should be clear and decisive. For example, when you read the following paragraph, do you know immediately the point of the paragraph? What is the writer's conclusion regarding the substance within this paragraph?

EXAMPLE A:

In *Milano,* the court held the evidence allowed a reasonable inference that the bar served the intoxicated driver alcohol despite the server's claim that she refused to sell him alcohol. 506 A.2d at 163, 164-65. The court reasoned the jury could have believed the driver entered the bar sober and left intoxicated where the driver got into an accident two blocks from the bar and was intoxicated at the scene of the accident. *Id.* at 165.

Now, read the following paragraph. Can you easily know the paragraph's point?

EXAMPLE B:

Even without direct evidence of a bar's sale to a patron, a jury could find that a sale occurred from circumstantial evidence. *Milano,* 506 A.2d at 165. For example, in *Milano,* the jury permissibly drew an inference that the bar sold to the intoxicated driver where the driver entered the bar sober and left intoxicated and got into an accident two blocks from the bar. *Id..* In addition, the driver was intoxicated at the scene of the accident, providing further circumstantial evidence from which the jury could infer that the bar sold alcohol to the driver. *Id..*

In example B, the writer decisively alerted the reader to the point of the paragraph. The sentence comfortably orients the reader. By contrast, in example A the writer begins with a case and the reader has no idea *why* that case is being discussed. The busy reader will react more favorably when the writer carefully walks the reader through the paragraph.

Here is how you might go about developing a paragraph's decisive and clear first sentence:

1. The idea emerges in draft form.

The New Hampshire courts look at the nature of the prior act when deciding on its admission. Cite.

> What does this tell the reader about how the rule works? (identifies nature of prior act as important)
> But what is it about the nature of the prior act that is important for the reader to understand?

2. The writer refines the point of the paragraph.

To determine the admissibility of a prior bad act, the New Hampshire courts analyze the relevance to the current charge. Cite.

> What does this tell the reader about how the rule works? (how relevant it is)
> What is missing? (connection to the overall rule's purpose)

3. The writer specifically identifies the purpose of the rule and the point of the paragraph with the opening sentence.

Courts determine whether a prior bad act is admissible by examining whether the prior act evidence is relevant because it specifically refutes the defendant's current defense. Cite. For example . . .

> What does this tell the reader about how the rule works? (relevance linked to refutation of defendant's defense)

4. The writer refines and sharpens the language, making the point precise and clear.

Evidence of a prior act is relevant to refute defendant's claim that the crime was committed by accident. Cite. For example in . . . .

Using Parallel Structure

Your analysis will be organized into paragraphs that explain the law followed by paragraphs that apply the law. Even though these paragraphs are doing different things, use the same structure in each. This will also help your reader to easily move through your analysis. In the paragraphs below, notice the parallel structure that is highlighted.

EXAMPLE: Explanation of law paragraph

The conclusion sentence: tells the reader the legal principle you are explaining.

Case information with illustrations.

The reasoning or rationale the court gives to justify its conclusion.

Evidence of a prior act is relevant to refute a defendant's claim that the crime was committed by accident. *Lesnick*, 677 A.2d at 690. For example, the court in *Lesnick* admitted evidence of a prior act because it was relevant to show the absence of an accident where the defendant claimed she had stabbed her husband in self-defense because she believed him to be an unknown intruder. *Id.* In contrast, where the defendant denied any involvement at all in the crime, the court excluded the evidence. *State v. Blackey*, 623 A.2d 1333, 1334 (N.H. 1993). It reasoned that the evidence was not relevant because, by denying the crime altogether, the defendant had not placed her intent or propensity at issue. *Id.* at 1334; *State v. Whittaker*, 642 A.2d 936, 938 (N.H. 1994).

EXAMPLE: Application of law paragraph

The conclusion sentence: tells the reader the legal principle you are applying to your client's facts.

Case information where illustrations are applied to client facts.

The reasoning or rationale the writer gives to justify legal conclusion.

Albert's prior act is likely relevant here because she claims she took the ham by accident. Like the defendant in *Lesnick*, who admitted the stabbing but claimed it was an accident, Albert made her intent an issue by claiming she took the ham unintentionally. Evidence of a prior similar act is relevant to disproving Albert's claim of accident because the two similar acts close in time indicate her intent to shoplift. Therefore, because the evidence of the prior act is offered for a purpose other than Albert's character or propensity to steal meat, it probably is admissible.

 Video Quiz

CHAPTER 10

Advanced Writing:
Multi-Issue Analysis

INTRODUCTION

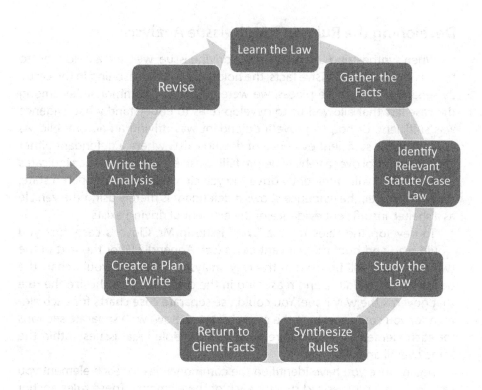

Sometimes a client's legal question requires you to write a multi-issue analysis within the same memo. Thus, this chapter expands on Mr. Clover's analysis. We provide an example of how to organize a memo where you must analyze more than one element, or sub-issue, of the client's legal question.

Assume, for example, that in addition to the driving analysis in Mr. Clover's case, your supervisor has asked you also to analyze whether the facts support that your client, Mr. Clover, was driving on a "way" in Magnolia. As you will recall, the Magnolia DUI statute requires proof of three elements to establish a defendant's guilt: (1) driving or attempting to drive; (2) on a way; and (3) under the influence. There is no question here that Mr. Clover was under the influence. The process of preparing to write the "way" analysis is largely the same as the process outlined for preparing to write the driving issue. You will still use the overall CREAC structure to analyze the "way" issue. Writing a memo that requires multi-issue analysis, however, requires a slightly different organization to help the reader fully understand the separate analysis of each element and how these elements relate to one another.

Developing the Rules in a Multi-Issue Analysis

When synthesizing the rules for the driving issue, we used a case chart to help us identify the decisive facts, the holding, and the reasoning in the cases. By separating out these pieces, we were able to see commonalities among the case law that allowed us to develop rules to understand what evidence was sufficient, or not, to prove a defendant was driving an automobile. As you will recall, sufficient evidence of driving exists where a defendant either exercises control over a vehicle before falling asleep, or the evidence indicates the defendant will imminently drive the vehicle while in his inebriated state. Where, however, the evidence shows a defendant is merely using the vehicle as a shelter, insufficient evidence of the element of driving exists.

To develop the rules for the "way" issue in Mr. Clover's case, first you would read and brief the relevant cases (see Appendix D for the text of the two cases that will be used in the way analysis). Then you would chart the decisive facts, holding, and reasoning in the case law to synthesize the rule that governs the way issue. You could use separate case charts for each element or you could combine the case chart (as below) with separate sections for each element when you are analyzing multiple legal issues within the same overall analysis.

Again, once you have identified the commonalities for each element you can develop a synthesized rule for each of the elements. These rules anchor your discussion of each element. We completed this type of exercise for the driving element. You need to synthesize a rule for the way element as well in preparation for writing your analysis of that issue.

Element:	Winstead	Holloran	O'Malley	Client facts
Driving	Decisive facts: Holding: Reasoning:	Decisive facts: Holding: Reasoning:	Decisive facts: Holding: Reasoning:	
	Krause	Peete		Client facts
Way	Decisive facts: Holding: Reasoning:	Decisive facts: Holding: Reasoning:		

PRACTICAL TIP

When writing a multi-issue analysis, be sure, when reading case law, that you properly identify which part of a case addresses which issue. While not the case in the sample memo here, sometimes a case that analyzes a particular crime in criminal law or cause of action in civil law analyzes multiple elements, factors, or other points that must be proved, of the analysis. For example, you might encounter a case that addresses both the driving and way elements in Magnolia. As a result, make sure when reading and analyzing a case, that you know what issues are addressed and use only the relevant part of the case when writing the analysis of that discrete issue. You will see discrete treatment of each sub-issue in the sample memo that starts on page 119.

The Roadmap Paragraph

Just like in a single-issue discussion section, a multi-issue discussion must also start with an overall roadmap paragraph that gives the reader an introduction of what is to come. Here is an example of an overall roadmap paragraph in a memo using Massachusetts law that explains when custodial interrogations trigger the requirement of *Miranda* warnings:

Connor can likely show that police subjected him to a custodial interrogation in the absence of adequate *Miranda* warnings. *Miranda* warnings are necessary for "custodial interrogations." *Miranda v. Arizona,* 384 U.S. 436, 444 (1966). Custodial interrogation is questioning initiated by law enforcement officers after a person has been taken into custody or otherwise deprived of his freedom of

The overall conclusion on the client's legal question.

action in any significant way. *Id.* There are four factors that determine whether an individual's freedom of action is sufficiently cur-
tailed such that *Miranda* warnings are required: (1) the place of the
interrogation; (2) whether the investigation has begun to focus on
the suspect, including whether there is probable cause to arrest the
suspect; (3) the nature of the interrogation, including whether the
interview was aggressive or, instead, informal and influenced in its
contours by the suspect; and (4) whether, at the time the incriminat-
ing statement was made, the suspect was free to end the interview
by leaving the locus of the interrogation or by asking the interroga-
tor to leave, as evidenced by whether the interview terminated with
the defendant's arrest. *Commonwealth v. Bryant,* 390 Mass. 729, 737
(1984). No one factor is conclusive. *Id.* Nor is there a specific formula
to be applied. *Commonwealth v. Haas,* 373 Mass. 545, 552 (1977).

The overall roadmap in a multi-issue analysis raises the sub-issues that will be discussed. It foreshadows the organization of the memo.

The remainder of the discussion section will be organized around each
of the four factors introduced in the roadmap. The discussion of each of the
factors includes its own CREAC analysis within the memo. Each section begins
with a mini-roadmap paragraph that gives the reader the rule on the sub-
issue (here the factors) being discussed in that section. The mini-roadmap
paragraph provides the rule for the sub-issue being analyzed. One reader-
friendly way to alert your reader that you will be explaining each sub-issue,
or factor, individually is to divide the sections of the discussion into parts that
have short headings. Here the headings could be:

1. Place of Interrogation
2. Focus of Investigation
3. Nature of Investigation
4. Suspect's Freedom to Leave

The paragraph below is an example of the mini-roadmap for the first factor, Place of Interrogation, under the *Miranda* analysis.

Place of Interrogation

Although Connor's questioning occurred in his apartment,
the court may still find that this rose to "custodial interrogation"
because there were six uniformed police officers present at the
time. Courts are concerned with interrogations that take place in
a police-dominated atmosphere. *Commonwealth v. Shine,* 398

Mass 641, 648 (1986). *See Miranda,* 384 U.S. at 445. Although it is less likely that the circumstances are custodial when the interrogation occurs in familiar surroundings, the courts will examine whether "a reasonable person in the defendant's circumstances would have found the setting isolating and coercive." *Breese v. Commonwealth,* 415 Mass. 249, 255 (1993); *Commonwealth v. Gallati,* 40 Mass. App. Ct. 111, 113 (1996).

PRACTICAL TIP

Think of subheadings as signposts written to alert the reader about which part of the overall rule the section, or individual CREAC, will address. Subheadings can be short, such as the example above, or they can be longer statements that state the Conclusion on the sub-issue. The sample Clover multi-issue memo (below) will illustrate longer sub-issue headings.

The paragraphs that follow each mini-roadmap paragraph will further explain the rule by using case illustrations or rule-based reasoning, as appropriate, and application of the law to the client's facts. Here is a visual of how the Discussion paragraphs in a multi-issue, objective memo could be organized:

OVERALL ROADMAP:

Sets out overall rule, including sub-issues. These might be elements, factors, or distinct parts of a rule.

Heading: Sub-element 1
Mini-roadmap of sub-element 1: Sets out rule pertaining to element, factor, or distinct part.
Explanation of sub-element 1: This may take more than one paragraph depending on how many cases you need to use to illustrate the rule or the complexity of the sub-issue.
Application of sub-element 1: As with the explanation paragraphs, this may take more than one paragraph depending on how many cases you need to use to illustrate the rule or the complexity of the sub-issue.
Conclusion on the sub-element 1: A sentence or two that restates the Conclusion only on the particular sub-issue being discussed.

Heading: Sub-element 2

Mini-roadmap of sub-element 2: Sets out rule pertaining to element, factor, or distinct part.

Explanation of sub-element 2: This may take more than one paragraph depending on how many cases you need to use to illustrate the rule or the complexity of the sub-issue.

Application of sub-element 2: As with the explanation paragraphs, this may take more than one paragraph depending on how many cases you need to use to illustrate the rule or the complexity of the sub-issue.

Conclusion on the sub-element 2: A sentence or two that restates the Conclusion only on the particular sub-issue being discussed.

Conclusion section: Overall Conclusion on the analysis of the two sub-issues.

Sample Multi-Issue Discussion Section

Assume now that your supervisor has asked you to analyze whether your client, Mr. Clover, was on a "way" when parked in the apartment complex in addition to analyzing whether he was "driving" under Magnolia law. The sample memo below builds upon the sample memo provided previously for the driving issue. The annotations identify where there are some differences between this sample and the single-issue sample in Mr. Clover's case already provided.

MEMORANDUM

To: Supervising Attorney
From: Student Associate
Date: July X, 20XX
Re: **Cleo Clover's DUI arrest—sufficiency of evidence for driving and way elements**

ISSUE

Under Magnolia Driving Under the Influence (DUI) law, did Mr. Clover "drive" on a "way" when he was found sleeping in the driver's seat of his car with the accessories in use but the engine off, in a private parking space of an apartment building's parking lot where he was not a resident?

SUMMARY

Likely yes. For purposes of Magnolia's DUI law, Mr. Clover was likely "driving" on a "way." Under the Magnolia DUI statute, Mr. Clover must drive on a way while under the influence of drugs or alcohol. There is no question that Mr. Clover was under the influence. Mr. Clover was driving because he had actual physical control of his car when he ignited the accessories in the vehicle while positioned in the driver's seat coming as close as possible to driving. He was on a "way" because the parking lot was paved, accessible from public streets, and no physical barriers precluded access to the lot.

FACTS

Mr. Clover is a software engineer who lives in Sweetwater, Magnolia. On Friday, October X, 20XX, at 2:00 a.m. Sweetwater Police Officer Lena Starling was patrolling through an apartment complex when she saw a car parked in a reserved space with the lights on and someone seated in the driver's seat. Upon closer inspection, the person was asleep with his head back in the driver's seat. Mr. Clover responded after Officer Starling knocked on his window twice, one time forcefully.

When Mr. Clover put his window down, Officer Starling was hit with an odor of alcohol, and further observed that Mr. Clover's eyes were bloodshot and that he appeared dazed. Officer Starling identified Mr. Clover through his license and registration and asked why he was sleeping in his car. Mr. Clover admitted he had been at an office party that ended sometime after midnight. Because he thought he was impaired, he asked his co-worker, Robin Branch, to drive him to her apartment where he could safely leave his car and walk or take an Uber the rest of the way home. He told Officer Starling he was worried someone might come and tow his car, so he stayed to "sleep it off."

Mr. Clover explained in an interview that Branch drove his car to her apartment complex and pulled into the paved parking lot right off the main road. An automatic arm gate existed at the entrance to the parking lot, but Branch indicated it was broken and had been stuck in the "up" position for the past year. As a result, visitors to residents of the complex frequently parked in the lot. A sign, however, indicated parking was for residents only and that all others would be towed.

Like the sample memo in Chapter 5, this memo has a proper heading with each section of the memo labeled.

This Issue contains the same 3 parts as the previous Issue statement: (1) the controlling law, (2) the specific legal question, and (3) the decisive facts. The decisive facts include facts pertaining to the "way" and "driving" elements.

This Summary includes the overall law with your conclusion and pertains to both sub-issues. The analysis weaves in sub rules (e.g., actual physical control) and decisive facts pertaining to both elements addressed in the memo.

The facts should include background or contextual facts and the decisive facts for both elements.

Both Branch and Mr. Clover got out of the car. Branch gave Mr. Clover his key fob and went into her building. As it was a chilly fall night, Mr. Clover put the key fob in his pocket and got back in the driver's seat of his car so he could be warm while accessing his Uber app on his phone. Once inside, he pressed the ignition button without pressing the brake to heat the car. Although the engine was not on, the car lights and heat were running. The car, a 2021 Toyota Highlander, turns on – the engine ignites – only if the key is nearby and the ignition button and brake are pushed in simultaneously. Otherwise with only a push of the ignition button (without pressing the brake), the accessories to the car can be used. Once the heat was on, Mr. Clover leaned his head back and fell asleep before he had completed calling for an Uber as navigating the app was taking longer than he wished due to poor cell service. Mr. Clover woke to Officer Starling's knocking.

When Mr. Clover was awake and identified, Officer Starling asked Mr. Clover to exit the car and complete three field sobriety tests. Mr. Clover failed these tests. Mr. Clover explained to Officer Starling that he had fallen asleep after giving up on summoning an Uber and that he figured he could move the car if the person whose spot he was in returned. Officer Starling placed Mr. Clover under arrest. At the station, Mr. Clover was given a blood test which showed his BAC at .11.

Mr. Clover has been charged with Driving Under the Influence and seeks our advice as to whether the State can prove its case against him.

DISCUSSION

Mr. Clover was likely driving a vehicle on a way under Magnolia's DUI statute because he was parked in a paved parking lot accessible from public streets, seated in the driver's seat of his car with the key fob in his pocket, the car lights and heat turned on, prepared to drive. A person violates the Magnolia DUI statute if they "drive or attempt to drive a vehicle upon any way of this state open to the public" while they are under the influence of drugs or alcohol. M.G. Rev. Stat. Ann. § 265-A:2 (2022). To meet the statute, three elements must be proved: (1) driving or attempting to drive; (2) on a way; and (3) under the influence. § 265-A:2. As Mr. Clover does not contest that he was under the influence, this memo will focus on whether he was "driving" upon a "way."

A. Mr. Clover was likely driving a vehicle under Magnolia's DUI statute because he was seated in the driver's seat with the key fob in his pocket, the car lights and heat turned on, prepared to drive.

Driving is defined as operation or being in "actual physical control" of the vehicle. *State v. Holloran*, 669 A.2d 800, 801 (M.G. 1995). The state can prove "actual physical control" if there is circumstantial evidence that the defendant had "the capacity bodily to guide or exercise dominion over the vehicle at the present time" before falling asleep, or that the defendant would "imminent[ly] operate" the vehicle. *State v. Winstead*, 836 A.2d 775, 778 (M.G. 2003); see also *Holloran*, 669 A.2d at 801-02. *But see State v. O'Malley*, 416 A.2d 1387, 1388 (M.G. 2002). "Actual physical control" differentiates between one using a vehicle as a shelter, and one who presents a public safety risk by exercising control of the vehicle while inebriated. *Holloran*, 669 A.2d at 801.

To prove actual physical control, the driver must have the capacity bodily to guide or exercise control over the vehicle. *Winstead*, 836 A.2d at 778. In *Winstead*,

---

This main roadmap is shorter than the one issue roadmap. It includes the overall Conclusion in the memo, the statutory rule, and dispenses with elements not discussed. Note that the subrules for each element move to the mini-roadmaps in the section discussing that element.

This heading shows: 1. the prediction on the element, and 2. provides the main reasons for that prediction.

This mini-roadmap contains the subrules defining driving and actual physical control. The rules move from broad to narrow in the paragraph.

The RE and RA illustrated here are the same as that printed in Chapter 8.

the defendant was found asleep and intoxicated upright in the driver's seat of his car, engine running, in a Wal-Mart parking lot. *Id.* at 776. The defendant testified that before falling asleep, he had unlocked the driver's side door, sat down, pressed the clutch, moved the car into neutral, started the engine, and turned on the heater. *Id.* at 778. Given the steps taken, and that starting the car comes "as close as possible" to operation, the court held that the defendant was in actual physical control of his vehicle before falling asleep. *Id.* (citing *Atkinson v. State*, 331 M.G. 199, 201 (M.G. 1993)).

Mr. Clover did exercise control over the vehicle because although the engine was not running, he took steps to put his body in a position to drive. Like the defendant in *Winstead* who testified to unlocking his car, pushing in the clutch, shifting to neutral, and turning the engine on to have the heat running, Mr. Clover fell asleep in the seated position, lights and heat running. Mr. Clover had to unlock and enter his car with his key fob nearby, push the ignition button and turn on the heat. Even though igniting the engine would take the extra step of pushing in the brake, Mr. Clover, like the defendant in *Winstead*, came as close to operation of the vehicle as possible by seating himself in the ready position and igniting the accessories with the key fob before he fell asleep. Thus, Mr. Clover exercised control over the car and as a result was in actual physical control of the vehicle.

Additionally, the state can use circumstantial evidence to show the driver will imminently operate the vehicle to prove actual physical control. *Winstead*, 836 A.2d at 778. For example, in *Holloran*, the defendant was legally parked on the side of the road, alone in the driver's seat with keys in the ignition. 669 A.2d at 800. Although the engine was off, the defendant stated that he was waiting for a call from his wife to pick her up with the keys in the ignition and his statements of intent to drive resulted in more than being "Parked While Intoxicated." *Id.* at 801. Instead, these facts show circumstantial evidence of imminent operation, and thus, the defendant presented "the hazard to which the drunk driving statute is directed" and was in actual physical control of his motor vehicle. *Id.*

Conversely, in *O'Malley*, the defendant was found asleep in the driver's seat of a friend's car, with the keys in the ignition, legally parked outside the friend's house. 416 A.2d at 1388. The defendant testified that he had hitchhiked to the friend's house. *Id.* The friend agreed to drive the defendant home and told him to go "warm-up" the car. *Id.* Finding this testimony "not unreasonable," the court held that there was not enough evidence to show imminent operation because "mere presence in a nonmoving vehicle" is insufficient to establish actual physical control. *Id.*

Mr. Clover was in actual physical control of his car because he declared his intention to move the vehicle. Like in *Holloran*, where the defendant's intention to pick up his wife in a neighboring town was enough to show actual physical control, Mr. Clover also indicated his intent to move the car should the resident whose spot he was in arrived. Similar to *Holloran*, although Mr. Clover's engine was off, his decision to remain in the vehicle without calling an Uber and his statement of intent to drive, even conditionally, is circumstantial evidence of imminent operation. However, unlike in *O'Malley*, where the defendant was warming up the car so a friend could drive him home, Mr. Clover did not call an

Uber or describe an alternative person or plan other than his intent to operate his vehicle. Even though Mr. Clover intended to "sleep it off" before he drove home, there is the possibility he would have to operate the vehicle while drunk, thereby presenting the type of "hazard" the drunk driving statute is trying to prevent. Mr. Clover's statement of imminent operation is more than being "Parked While Intoxicated" and thus, he likely had actual physical control over his vehicle.

This heading includes the prediction on the "way" element and the key reasons for that prediction.

B. Mr. Client was likely on a way under Magnolia's DUI statute because the parking space was paved, easily accessible from public streets, and used by members of the public.

The mini-roadmap for the "way" element includes the statutory language. It then moves from broad to narrow in defining the term. The mini-roadmap also incorporates some policy.

Under the Magnolia DUI statute, which applies to both private- and publicly-owned roadways, a "way of this state open to the public" is one that is "adapted and fitted for public travel and in common use by the public." *State v. Krause*, 480 A.3d 224, 228 (M.G. 2021); *City of Aspen v. Peete*, 729 A.2d 1268, 1269 (M.G. 1987). In determining if a way is "adapted and fitted for public travel and in common use by the public," a court should consider the surrounding circumstances, such as the physical condition of the way, how difficult or easy it is for the public to gain access to the way, the way's location, and its history of use. *See Krause*, 480 A.3d at 228; *Peete*, 729 A.2d at 1270-71. If the overall circumstances indicate a member of the public is likely to use the way, Magnolia's impaired driving laws will apply to the way. *Krause*, 480 A.3d at 228.

A way is "adapted and fitted for public travel and in common use by the public" if it is paved, there are limited restrictions on its use, it is easily accessible from other public roadways, and members of the public use the way. *See Krause*, 480 A.3d at 228; *Peete*, 729 A.2d at 1270-71. For example, in *Krause*, a defendant found sitting in a car in a parking spot allocated to residents of a nearby public housing complex was on a "way of this state open to the public." 480 A.3d at 228. The parking spot was easily accessible from public streets. *Id.* Nothing physically prevented a member of the public from driving into the parking area, although a sign indicated that the parking area was for tenants only and that violators would be towed. *Id.* at 225, 228. The court reasoned, in addition, that the parking area was part of a public housing complex, located near a public park, and the defendant, a member of the public and not a resident of the housing complex, was using the parking space, all of which indicated the space was a public way under the statute. *Id.* at 228.

Here are two RE paragraphs explaining the Krause case and the Peete case being used in the way analysis. Note that there is one statement of law or thesis sentence for both cases that synthesizes the rule from them. The case illustrations include the facts, holding, and reasoning of each case.

Similarly, in *Peete*, the court held that the defendant was driving on a public way when he had his accident. 729 A.2d at 1269, 1270-71. The intoxicated defendant was driving in a private hotel parking garage, where he rented a monthly space, when he hit a motorcycle. *Id.* at 1269. Parking in the garage was available both for short-term visitors and monthly renters. *Id.* Short-term parking required obtaining a ticket from a parking attendant and paying a fee upon leaving the garage; monthly renters paid a monthly fee and came and went from the garage at will. *Id.* The court reasoned that the parking area was paved and required only payment of a fee to use it, making restriction to the area minimal. *Id.* at 1270. Moreover, the public frequently used the parking lot, and was encouraged to use it. *Id.* Under the circumstances, the court held that the private parking "facility [was] obviously fitted for public travel and in common use by the public." *Id.* at 1270-71.

The parking lot in Mr. Clover's case is likely "adapted and fitted for public travel and in common use by the public" because it is paved, easily accessible from public streets, there are only limited restrictions on its use, and members of the public, such as visitors of residents of the apartment complex, use the lot. Like the parking garage in *Peete*, which was paved, the parking lot here is paved. Just like both the parking garage in *Peete* and the parking spot in *Krause* were easily accessible from public streets, the parking lot in Mr. Clover's case is also easily accessible from public streets. Branch turned into the lot from a main street. Moreover, as seen in *Krause*, a sign like the one here that simply says spaces are reserved for tenants and that violators will be towed is not a sufficient restriction on its use to indicate a way is not public under the DUI statute. In addition, like the defendant in *Krause*, who did not live in the apartment complex but was able to access the parking space, here Mr. Clover was found parked in a spot in the lot, all of which indicates it is likely a public way.

This RA paragraph for the way analysis starts by applying the rule stated in the thesis of the RE paragraph to the facts of Mr. Clover's case. The paragraph further contains case comparisons and an application of the law to the Clover facts.

Mr. Clover might argue that the presence of the gate arm indicates some intention to discourage members of the public from using the lot or that the gate arm is a physical barrier to entering the lot. Unlike the garage in *Peete* where members of the public were encouraged to use the lot and there was no physical barrier to entry, here the existence of the gate arm could signal intention to discourage public use. Because the gate is broken, however, no barrier to accessing the lot actually exists, and the owners of the complex have not fixed the gate for the past year indicating they are not overly concerned about public use. Mr. Clover could have accessed the spot himself simply by driving into the lot, and there is evidence that visitors to the complex readily access the parking lot when visiting residents. As a result, it is unlikely the mere existence of the broken gate arm is enough to persuade a court that the lot is not a public way. The parking lot is paved, close to public streets, and members of the public have unimpeded access to the area. The surrounding circumstances indicate members of the public are entitled to protection from impaired drivers when using the way, and, as a result, Mr. Clover was likely on a public way when arrested by Officer Starling.

This RA paragraph illustrates a way to address factual counter-analysis in a memo. The broken automatic arm at the parking lot entrance in Mr. Clover's case is a factual difference that should be addressed.

CONCLUSION

Mr. Clover was likely driving as he was seated in the driver's seat with the key fob in his pocket, with the heat on, and he indicated he would imminently operate his car. He was likely on a way because he was parked in a paved parking space that was accessible from public streets and frequently used by members of the public. As a result, Mr. Clover is likely guilty of DUI under Magnolia law.

Note that this overall Conclusion addresses both elements, not just driving.

Summary of Differences in One-Issue versus Two-Issue Discussion Section

The main differences between a Discussion section that analyzes one sub-issue and a Discussion section that addresses two sub-issues primarily involve the Rule sections and the overall organization of the Discussion section. In a single-issue memo, the main roadmap will likely be a bit longer than in a multi-issue memo. This is because the subrules for each sub-issue will move to the mini-roadmaps for each CREAC in the memo. With a single-issue memo, the subrules are included in the main roadmap paragraph.

In addition, the multi-issue memo will have multiple CREACs in it rather than just one, as in a single-issue memo. As you can see from looking at the above example memo, there is a separate CREAC for both the driving issue and the way issue. Each sub-issue needs its own discrete, focused analysis.

CHAPTER 11

Counter-Analysis

INTRODUCTION

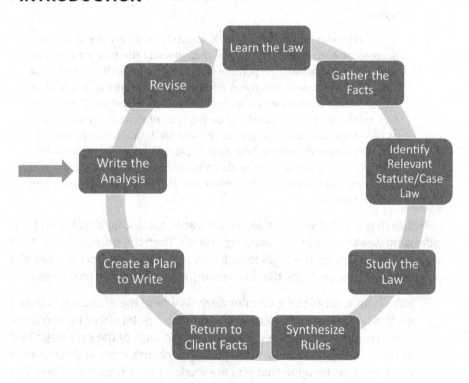

The purpose of a counter-analysis is to let your reader know about the potential weaknesses in your prediction and how you will address them. You should have an idea about what the opposing counsel might argue or what a court might have concerns about. The counter-analysis lets your reader know that you have looked at the law and the facts from all angles and have ideas about how to approach weaknesses and any opposing arguments. Including a counter-analysis will give your reader assurance that your thinking is thorough, deep, and has left no stone unturned.

FACT AND LAW-BASED COUNTER-ANALYSIS

There are different ways to incorporate a counter-analysis. The focus might be fact-based, where the facts of a relevant case you are using present an alternative analysis. Another type of counter-analysis is law-based, where a particular case's law or policy presents a potential alternative outcome in your client's case. Here are examples of these approaches:

- Here is the counter-analysis in the sample memo on page 8. In this approach the counter-analysis is based on the law—here it's a policy relied on by the court. Using a parenthetical, the author is noting that the policy supporting the law may form the basis of an opposing analysis.

> Albert's only argument in her favor likely relies on the underlying purpose of 404(b). She could argue that allowing the bad act evidence against her goes against the purpose behind 404(b) and its limitations. *Id.* at 1195 (holding purpose underlying rule 404(b) is to ensure that a defendant is tried on the merits of the case and not on character). However, the concern that a defendant not be convicted on the basis of character is met where, as here, there is a sufficient, specific purpose for its admission. By claiming that she mistakenly took the ham, Albert's placed her own intent to commit theft at issue. The prosecutor would probably be successful in arguing that the purpose of the evidence is to refute that claim and not to demonstrate her bad character.

Notice that the first sentence alerts the reader specifically that the writer is addressing weaknesses or opposing arguments. Then the potential argument is laid out, followed by the legal foundation that might support it. Next, the writer explains how and why the counter-argument is unlikely to succeed.

- Here is an example of a counter-analysis where the approach is **based on facts**—the author is demonstrating how a potential opposing argument could be made based on applying the facts of the case described in the rule explanation to the facts of the client's case. In the example memo below, imagine that you are working for a prosecutor, and you have been asked to write a memo predicting whether a defendant, who is charged with gun possession, can successfully move to suppress the gun on grounds that it was recovered by the police after an illegal stop and search. After researching the law, you have concluded that the police acted lawfully. This is the discussion section of the memo:

Overall Roadmap paragraph.

> The police likely acted reasonably under art. 14 of the Massachusetts Constitution and the Fourth Amendment where they made a limited pat

frisk of Carter after receiving information that Carter "displayed" a firearm at an after-hours party and yelled to bystanders he would be back. Under art. 14 of the Massachusetts Constitution and the Fourth Amendment, police officers act reasonably when they stop and frisk a suspect after receiving information that the suspect is in possession of a firearm when the circumstances indicate a concern for public safety. *Commonwealth v. Foster*, 724 N.E.2d 357, 361 (Mass. App. Ct. 2000). An informant's report that a suspect is carrying a gun, without any other indicia of danger to police or the public, is not enough to justify a stop and frisk. *Commonwealth v. Couture*, 552 N.E.2d 538, 540 (Mass. 1990). However, when the circumstances give rise to public safety concerns, the police have a duty to investigate a tip of gun possession "and may perform a pat frisk if they have a reasonable belief that the defendant is 'armed and dangerous.'" *Foster*, 724 N.E.2d at 359-60.

Massachusetts courts have upheld a suspect's stop and pat frisk where the tip came from a known or anonymous source, concerned firearms possession, and indicated the suspect presented a danger to public safety. *Commonwealth v. Johnson*, 631 N.E.2d 71, 72 (Mass. App. Ct. 1994); *Commonwealth v. McCauley*, 419 N.E.2d 1072, 1073 (Mass. App. Ct. 1981). For example, in *Johnson*, the court upheld a pat frisk where a known citizen informed police a suspect was carrying a gun, and the suspect was shouting obscenities and gesticulating in an angry manner. 631 N.E.2d at 72. In *McCauley*, the court upheld a pat frisk based on an anonymous tip where the suspect was in a well-filled café at a late hour, may have been intoxicated, and had dropped his firearm repeatedly on the floor. 419 N.E.2d at 1073. The *McCauley* court noted that "the [late] hour, the location of the inquiry, the risks to other patrons, and the specificity of the anonymous report describing McCauley" justified the police officers' actions. *Id.*

Reasonableness is at the center of any art. 14 of the Massachusetts Constitution or Fourth Amendment analysis regarding governmental intrusion of a person's body. *Id.* Where, as in *Johnson* and *McCauley*, the suspects by their conduct and manner presented a danger to others, the police had a duty to investigate a tip regarding firearm possession from a known informant or, as in *McCauley*, from an anonymous informant, where the tip was specific enough to warrant reliance upon it. *Johnson*, 631 N.E.2d at 72; *McCauley*, 419 N.E.2d at 1073. Thus, the police acted reasonably in both cases when they performed a limited pat frisk of each defendant to uncover a weapon. *Johnson*, 631 N.E.2d at 72; *McCauley*, 419 N.E.2d at 1073.

If the informant's tip merely informs police that a suspect possesses a firearm, without an indication of a threat or risk to the public, a stop and frisk is not justified. *Couture*, 552 N.E.2d at 541. In *Couture*, a store clerk called police and informed them that a customer had entered his store and "had a small handgun protruding from his right rear pocket." *Id.* at 539. Police subsequently stopped the customer based on the clerk's report of the customer's license plate, ordered him out of his truck, searched his vehicle, and discovered a .38 caliber pistol under the front seat. *Id.* In suppressing the evidence, the court reasoned the tip provided no evidence that the customer acted suspiciously in the store. *Id.* at 540. He did not threaten or intimidate the clerk; nor did he linger suspiciously or act like he was "casing the joint" to commit a robbery. *Id.* The

Explanation of the law using facts, holding, and reasoning from case law.

Explanation of the law using facts, holding, and reasoning from case law.

Explanation of the law using facts, holding, and reasoning from case law.

only information police knew from the tip was that the customer possessed a gun in a public place. *Id.* As a result, without more, the officers' stop and seizure of the defendant, his vehicle, and his gun were unlawful where nothing indicated the customer was about to engage in illegal activity. *Id.* at 541.

Here the police likely acted reasonably when they pat frisked Carter based on the known informant's tip because the circumstances surrounding the tip likely indicated that Carter posed a threat to public safety. Like the *McCauley* case, where the police received a tip that *McCauley* had displayed a firearm late at night when he may have been intoxicated, Carter displayed a firearm in public after leaving a party in the early morning. The police in *Johnson* also acted reasonably in pat frisking the defendant after receiving a tip from a known informant that she was carrying a gun and acting belligerently. Similarly, the police here acted reasonably in pat frisking Carter because he "displayed" a firearm at an early morning hour and yelled to bystanders that he would be back. In fact, the police had a duty to investigate here, just like in the precedent cases, because the circumstances, including the defendant's conduct and the early hour, indicated a threat to public safety. Like the police officers in *Johnson* and *McCauley*, who acted reasonably under the circumstances when they made a limited pat frisk of individuals who posed a threat to the public, the police likely acted reasonably here and complied with art. 14 of the Massachusetts Constitution and the Fourth Amendment when they made a limited pat frisk of Carter based on information from a known informant that he posed a threat to public safety.

Carter may argue that his case is like *Couture* in that there was no information other than his public possession of a firearm without any threat. This would make the stop and frisk unreasonable under the circumstances and a violation of his rights under art. 14 of the Massachusetts Constitution and the Fourth Amendment. This argument will likely fail. In *Couture*, other than the store clerk's statement that he saw the customer with a gun, there existed no additional indicia that created a concern for public safety. As the court noted in *Couture*, despite wearing the gun on his person, the defendant did not act suspiciously in the store. However, in *McCauley*, the court relied on "the [late] hour, the location of the inquiry, the risks to other patrons, and the specificity of the anonymous report describing McCauley" to justify the police officers' actions. Similarly, in the instant case, the hour was late, several people were still at the party when Carter displayed his weapon and indicated he would be back, and the tip from the informant described what Carter was wearing and in which direction he had headed after leaving the party.

The sample memo in our DUI case on page 77 is another example of a fact-based counter-analysis. In the paragraph below excerpted from the memo, the author uses the *Peete* facts to alert the reader of a potential argument the defendant could make regarding whether the parking area was a "way" under the statute. The author then shows the reader why this argument is not likely to succeed.

Mr. Clover might argue that the presence of the gate arm indicates some intention to discourage members of the public from using the lot or that the gate arm is a physical barrier to entering the lot. Unlike the garage in *Peete* where members of the public were encouraged to use the lot and there was no physical barrier to entry, here the existence of the gate arm could signal intention to discourage public use. Because the gate is broken, however, no barrier to accessing the lot actually exists, and the owners of the complex have not fixed the gate for the past year indicating they are not overly concerned about public use. Mr. Clover could have accessed the spot himself simply by driving into the lot, and there is evidence that visitors to the complex readily access the parking lot when visiting residents. As a result, it is unlikely the mere existence of the broken gate arm is enough to persuade a court that the lot is not a public way. The parking lot is paved, close to public streets, and members of the public have unimpeded access to the area. The surrounding circumstances indicate members of the public are entitled to protection from impaired drivers when using the way, and, as a result, Mr. Clover was likely on a public way when arrested by Officer Starling.

WHERE DOES A COUNTER-ANALYSIS GO IN A MEMO?

A counter-analysis can be integrated in the application as part of the "A" in IRAC (or CREAC). The examples above demonstrate this organization.

You can also introduce a new case after the main explanation and application, introducing the counter-analysis in a separate explanation (with cites)/application paragraph. This structure is useful if you have a case that you believe presents strong support for the opposing side's position. Here is an example of what this type of counter-analysis would look like. This one is based on our texting client's case from Chapter 7.

Imagine that you are a prosecutor and you have charged the defendant, who was checking for directions on a phone application, with violating the new statute. A new case (Case D) has been decided where the court held that checking Instagram while walking on a public street is not a violation of the statute. You are writing a memorandum where you discuss the strength of the case against the defendant. In the memo, you discuss Cases A, B, and C in the rule explanation and application. Rather than discussing Case D in the rule explanation and application, you address the case separately after the rule explanation and application of the other cases. This lets the reader know that there is an important new case offering a potential strong defense, but you have considered the case and you believe that it will not change the outcome:

> Defendant may rely on the recently decided Case D where the court held that reading Instagram on a phone is insufficient "communication with another person" to violate the statute. CITE. In Case D the court reasoned that while checking Instagram potentially includes a type of communication with another individual, it is less distracting because the communication does not necessarily involve a contemporaneous response. CITE. Here, Client may argue that checking a map or directions is similar to checking Instagram in that there is no response called for

contemporaneously. However, this argument will likely fail. Checking directions, while not communication with another, is contemporaneous in the sense that the client had an immediate need to know the information, unlike an Instagram communication where there is not necessarily an immediate response needed, which makes it less distracting than checking directions as in Case B (playing a game). Thus, a court would likely find that the safety concerns noted in case A and C would apply in Client's case.

Effective Counter-Analysis—Do's and Don'ts

- Use words or phrases to alert the reader that you are shifting to the counter-analysis. In the example above, the writer does this by saying, "Carter may argue that . . ." Words to alert the reader include "although," "on the other hand," or "despite."
- Be specific about the factual basis and legal grounds for a counter-analysis.
  Not helpful: Carter may argue that the police acted unreasonably in stopping and frisking him.
  Helpful: Carter may argue that his case is like *Couture*, and that there was no information other than his public possession of a firearm without any threat. This would make the stop and frisk unreasonable under the circumstances and would violate his rights under art. 14 of the Massachusetts Constitution and the Fourth Amendment.
- Include the legal support for the counter-analysis. Notice in the example above that the writer shows how the *Couture* case could be used to support a different legal conclusion.
- Specifically refute the counter-analysis. Show the reader how you would deal with the opposing position. In the example above, the reader is clear about this when she says, "This argument will likely fail." She follows this with the specific reasons why it will fail.

CHAPTER 12

Client Letters and Emails

INTRODUCTION

Client letters can cover many topics, but there are two common types: a retainment letter and a letter summarizing the legal issues and probable outcome of your client's case. Retainment letters tend to be formulaic and practice-specific. In this chapter we will focus on client letters and emails that contain substantive content about the case. The example in Appendix A is the second type, where the lawyer explains the probable outcome of a client's case.

Emails and letters to another lawyer or client summarizing the legal issues and probable outcome of a case will typically serve the same purpose as a legal memorandum—to offer an objective analysis. The content will be similar to a legal memorandum. Client letters can be emails, hard copy, or both. Whether the letter is in an email or hard copy, there is a helpful common structure based on IRAC.

CLIENT LETTERS AND EMAILS

Organization—Long Form

A client letter that gives a client a prediction in his or her case follows the basic IRAC structure that you are now used to. Below is an example with labels and annotations in the margin to identify the IRAC (or CREAC) structure.

Carla Client
3 West Street
Town, State

Re: Liz Baker's Law Degree as Marital Property

<table>
<tr><td>Issue or question presented. Notice that the last sentence gives a prediction (or conclusion).</td><td>As requested, this letter will give you my opinion about whether your former wife's law degree and its attendant monetary value are marital property under our state's law. I have studied the relevant law in relation to your facts. Since you and Liz jointly decided that she should attend law school, the degree and its value is likely marital property. The valuation of the degree will have to be assessed by an expert and therefore this letter will not address that issue.</td></tr>
</table>

Explanation of Relevant Law

Rule and explanation. Notice how the law is explained in a layperson's terms. There are no references to cases or statutes, and no citations.

Marital property means all property acquired by spouses during the marriage. Earned degrees generally constitute marital property where the couple jointly decides how to develop their future earning capacity to support their family by sending one party to school. Our courts view marriage as a partnership and, when a marriage ends, each of the spouses, based on the totality of the contributions made to it, has a stake in and right to a share of the marital property. This is because that property represents the capital product of the partnership.

In long-term marriages where the parties jointly decide how to raise their family, manage their future earning capacity, and share expectations of future material benefit, the court usually awards a sum representing the fair distribution of the professional degree. The court will also consider the sacrifices made by a spouse without a professional degree. When a supporting spouse sacrifices a career or makes a significant financial contribution toward the spouse's professional education, expecting both parties to enjoy material benefits from the degree, the court will likely view the degree as marital property.

The Likely Outcome of This Issue

Application of the law to the client's specific facts.

You will likely be awarded a sum representing a fair distribution of Liz's law degree. You and Liz have a long-term marriage and you decided together that she would get her degree first while you managed the home and the children. In addition, you sacrificed by putting off attending graduate school. Because you and Liz jointly agreed on this course of action for the benefit of the family, the court will likely award you a fair distribution of the degree. Liz's attorney will likely argue that the future monetary value is uncertain and unquantifiable. However, the court has rejected this argument in cases similar to yours. Moreover, the court will likely accept our position if we have a credible expert to calculate the degree's value.

Conclusion and Next Steps

Conclusion and follow-up steps.

Based on my preliminary research, it appears that Liz's law degree will be a marital asset. Our next step is to discuss hiring an expert to value the degree. These experts can be expensive, so we should discuss whether you want to pursue this course. I suggest sending Liz's lawyer a letter outlining our position on her law degree. Perhaps we can resolve this aspect of your divorce through negotiation and agreement. Let me know if you have any questions or concerns.

Sincerely,
Lawyer

Organization—Short Form

An email to a client or another lawyer could also be shorter than a legal memorandum, depending on the circumstances. A short version typically shrinks the rule explanation and makes use of parentheticals with citations. It might also include bulleted conclusions. On the next page you will see an example of what that might look like in the case of Mr. Clover if a colleague (another lawyer) had asked you to research whether Mr. Clover was "driving" under the Magnolia DUI statute.

From: JD Roy, Associate
To: Robin Wren, Supervising Attorney
Subject Line: Whether Mr. Clover was "driving" under Magnolia's DUI law

Robin,

At your request, I researched whether Mr. Clover was "driving" under Magnolia's Driving Under the Influence statute.

Mr. Clover was likely "driving" under Magnolia's DUI statute because he was in the driver's seat of his car with the key fob in his pocket, the car lights and heat turned on, and he stated he intended to drive soon.

A person violates the Magnolia DUI statute if they "drive or attempt to drive a vehicle upon the ways of this state open to the public" while they are under the influence of drugs or alcohol. M.G. Rev. Stat. Ann. § 265-A:2 (2022). Driving is defined as operation or being in "actual physical control" of the vehicle. *State v. Holloran*, 669 A.2d 800, 801 (M.G. 1995).

The state can prove "actual physical control" if there is circumstantial evidence that the defendant had "the capacity bodily to guide or exercise dominion over the vehicle at the present time" before falling asleep or that the defendant would imminently operate the vehicle. *State v. Winstead*, 836 A.2d 775, 776 (M.G. 2003) (holding the defendant was in actual physical control where he was asleep and intoxicated, sitting in the driver's seat of his running car, and before falling asleep, had unlocked the driver's side door, pressed in the clutch to shift into neutral, started the engine, and turned on the heater).

Circumstantial evidence that the driver will imminently operate the car is also enough to prove actual physical control. *Holloran*, 669 A.2d at 801 (holding that actual physical control includes being as close to operating the car without actual driving where the defendant was awake in the driver's seat with the keys in the ignition and the engine off, and he said he was waiting for a call from his wife to pick her up in another town after a party). However, actual physical control is not supported if the defendant had no plan to set the car in motion. *State v. O'Malley*, 416 A.2d 1387, 1388 (M.G. 2002) (holding that defendant was not in actual physical control where defendant's friend had agreed to drive defendant home and told defendant to "warm up" the car even though defendant fell asleep in the driver's seat of the friend's car, with the keys in the ignition).

Conclusion and Recommendation:

Mr. Clover was likely "driving" under Magnolia's statute. Mr. Clover was in the driver's seat with the car engine partially on—the heat and electrical systems were operational. Mr. Clover had the key fob in his pocket and had planned to move the car if the tenant whose parking space the car was reserved for returned. Although the engine was not running, the car was partially on, indicating that Mr. Clover was close to operatiing without actually driving the car.

I have attached the relevant cases. Please let me know if you need further research or for me to draft any responses to a pleading.

Regards,
JD

Margin annotations:

Brief identification of the issue being addressed. This is the shortened version of the "I" in IRAC.

Bolded conclusion giving reader the condensed answer. Similar to a Brief Answer in a Memo.

Starts with overall rule (the "R" in IRAC).

Paragraph starts with rule (the "R" in IRAC). Parenthetical description of case instead of a full rule explanation of *Winstead*. This is the shortened version the rule explanation (RE).

Paragraph starts with rule (the "R" in IRAC).

Parenthetical description of cases instead of a full rule explanation of *Holloran* and *O'Malley*. This is the shortened version the rule explanation (RE).

Short paragraph applying the client's facts to the rules and cases above, but without specifically applying the cases. This is the shortened version of the "A" in IRAC.

Style and Format

Your reader may be another lawyer, a government official, a businessperson, or a layperson. Frequently, several people with varying backgrounds may read your letter, for example, a board of directors, a group of small business owners, or planning board members. Write so that your reader(s) can understand you. Keep in mind that client letters also serve as a helpful summary of the case. If you are working on a complex case that stretches over a long period of time, the client letters are helpful tools for recalling what has happened in the case.

Tailor your tone to your relationship with the client. Be respectful, specific, and candid. Keep in mind that you are a professional; do not use slang or "text speak," but be direct.

Write in plain English, avoid legalese, and keep sentences short and concise. Use short paragraphs. Your reader should understand your writing without asking for a translator. Avoid all ambiguities.

TIPS ON PROFESSIONAL EMAIL COMMUNICATION

Lawyers communicate primarily by email, whether it is with a client, another lawyer, or another professional. You will likely communicate with prospective employers via email as early as the winter of your first year in law school. In law school, you will email your professors, the law school staff, and fellow students. Here are a few rules of the road to follow:

1. ***Email with your professors and the law school staff.*** Treat all communication with law school personnel (faculty and staff) as professional correspondence. This is a good time to practice good habits. Here are some guidelines:
   - Identify the content of the email with a proper subject line. Do not find an old email with an unrelated subject and reply to it without changing the subject line. Format the subject line properly. Use capital letters and a brief (one to four words) description of the email's nature.
   - Use a proper salutation, as in "Dear Professor Carter" or "Dear Ms. Jones" (if it is a staff member).
   - Use proper English in the body of the email. Do not use abbreviations, slang, or text speak. Do not be overly formal or use legal jargon.
   - Proofread carefully. It will matter to your recipient and reflect poorly on your abilities if you send an email with typos or misspellings.
   - Be respectful and deferential in your tone.

2. ***Email with clients or other lawyers.*** Your search for a summer placement may begin sometime in the second semester. You will likely begin communicating with other lawyers via email in your first year of law school. Once in a summer placement, you may be asked to draft an email to a client or another lawyer. Apply the rules above to these types of emails. Follow the guidelines on client letters above and apply them to email correspondence. They will be structured the same, except that the address and contact information should be part of the signature. In addition, you will want to include a confidentiality statement as part of the signature block. Check with your employer about the proper contents of your signature block.

A typical email signature is shown on the next page.

Susan Barkley

sbarkley@workemail.com
623-233-1234 direct
623-233-2333 main
Barkley Law Offices
7 Hathaway St
Anytown, NY 23456

Confidentiality Notice: This message is intended only for the person to whom addressed in the text above and may contain privileged or confidential information. If you are not that person, any use of this message is prohibited. We request that you notify us by replying to this message and then delete all copies, including any contained in your reply. Thank you.

Most employers have an email and Internet policy; you should ask to see it once you begin your employment. Employers have the right to read your work emails and monitor your Internet usage, and most do. Moreover, your emails may become the subject of a request that a litigant asks for as part of a discovery process. Thus, when you draft an email, consider that your audience may be wider than the recipient. Your reputation, credibility, and ability are all at stake with just about every legal correspondence you author. Use the *New York Times* rule on emailing (also known as the "Front Page of the Newspaper" Test): "Don't do anything you wouldn't want published on the front page of the *New York Times*."

CHAPTER 13

Revising

INTRODUCTION

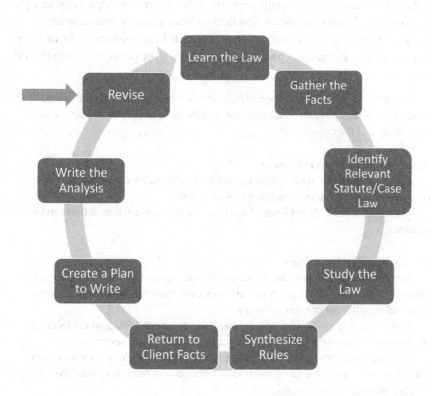

Learn the Law

Gather the Facts

Identify Relevant Statute/Case Law

Study the Law

Synthesize Rules

Return to Client Facts

Create a Plan to Write

Write the Analysis

Revise

Revising makes up a large percentage of the writing process. The different kinds of revising—large-scale, internal paragraph, and micro (grammar and mechanics)—will be discussed in this chapter. Your education may have included grammar training, but conventions have changed. Make your writing as accessible as possible. For example, one convention that has changed is the use of pronouns. To be inclusive, avoid referring to "he or she" as a construct.

The tips in this chapter will give you some tools to tighten and sharpen your language. The goal is to consider your reader and to make your writing respectful, clear, and concise.

LARGE-SCALE REVISING

One way to check if your analysis has a solid organization is to deconstruct it. Here is a strategy for assessing your organization.

Highlight each paragraph's first sentence or cut and paste each first sentence into a separate document. Each sentence, standing alone, should logically show the layout of your argument. If one of the sentences lacks a clear focus, it will interrupt the logical flow of your stand-alone sentences.

Look at the sentences below. They are the first sentences from each paragraph in the sample on page 9. Notice how they present an organized logic.

Albert's prior act involving the turkey is relevant for a purpose other than character because she raised the issue of intent, and the prior act is factually similar and close in time to the charged act.

Direct Bearing on Issue in Dispute
Evidence of a prior act is relevant to refute a defendant's claim that the crime was committed by accident. *Lesnick*, 677 A.2d at 690.

Albert's prior act is likely relevant here because she claims she took the ham by accident.

Clear and Logical Connection
Next, the evidence probably meets the second prong of the relevancy analysis because a clear, logical connection exists between the charged act of stealing a ham and the prior act of taking a turkey.

Where two acts are significantly different, the court will not admit evidence of the first one to prove the defendant's intent in committing the second act.

In Albert's case, the turkey and the ham were similar products removed from the same store, using the same method of removal—all facts that show that the second incident was not an accident.

Moreover, the close time frame between Albert's two incidents further strengthens their connection.

INTERNAL PARAGRAPH REVISING

One tool for checking and revising paragraphs is the reverse outline. Reverse outlining will help you practice critically reading and evaluating what you have written so that you can make your document more effective. This strategy gives you the real picture of your argument **as it is currently written**. By naming what you have done and seeing the document in its true skeletal form, you can get a better perspective on what is on the page and how you can start to make it more effective. *This is a technique you can use for any writing to ensure that what you have written is what you meant to say and to see how the parts of the writing work together.*

1. First, read the entire section (sub-issue) without stopping.
2. Re-read and note what is **actually present** in the writing (not what you think *should* be there or what you plan to have there or what was in your initial outline—unless that is exactly what *is* there). Describe what you see. In particular, note if you see the explanation of law or application of client facts to law.
3. Note the overall point of each paragraph.
4. Note the point of each sentence in the paragraph.
5. Read the reverse outline, looking for:
   - **Organization.** Does the structure of the discussion section work logically? Is it set out in a way that the reader can follow?
   - **Content.** Do the authorities "flesh out" the analysis? Do the authorities fully show the analysis?
   - **Depth of analysis.** Are cases summarized/synthesized before being described individually? Are the authorities analyzed around principles? Are decisive facts, holding, and reasoning noted where appropriate? Are facts analogized and distinguished?
   - **Gaps and ambiguities.** Having reverse outlined the section, what gaps do you notice? Do the paragraphs include transitions and show how they relate? Does each paragraph have one main point? Do the parts of the analysis have introductory road maps? Are there inconsistencies? Are the assumptions appropriate?

MICRO REVISING: GRAMMAR AND MECHANICS

Law students juggle many new concepts as they master legal writing, which can lead to cognitive overload. Here is a list of tips and tools to use as a reference.

1. **Generally, avoid passive voice.**
   - A "be" verb plus a past participle (a verb ending in –ed) can indicate passive voice.

> **EXAMPLE:** *Is dismissed; are docketed; was vacated = passive voice.*

- what to whom in this sentence?" Then rewrite the sentence to focus on the actor, the action, and the object (if there is an object).
- The word "by" can indicate passive voice.

> **EXAMPLE:** *The sentence was commuted by the governor* **versus** *The governor commuted the sentence.*

> **EXAMPLE: Sentence with passive voice**
>
> *The four factors <u>to be</u> taken into account in <u>considering</u> a request for the entry of a preliminary injunction are . . .*

> **EXAMPLE: Same sentence edited**
>
> *A court considers four factors in deciding whether to impose a preliminary injunction. The factors are . . .*

2. Omit unnecessary words
   - Replace four or five words with one or two.

> **EXAMPLE: Too many words**
>
> *The fact that the court repeatedly ruled against the defendant was evidence of its bias.*

> **EXAMPLE: Omitting the excess**
>
> *The court's repeated denials of the defendant's objections indicated its bias.*

3. Use base verbs, not nominalizations
   - Legal readers want you to be clear and concrete. Use verbs to describe the action.

> **EXAMPLE:** *Act* **versus** *action; conclude* **versus** *making conclusions.*

- A nominalization is a verb turned into a noun. You can spot a nominalization by its ending. Endings associated with nominalizations include:

-al	-ment	-ant	-ence
-ion	-ent	-ancy	-ency
-ance	-ity		

> **EXAMPLE:** *The defendant's request is that his sentence be reduced* **versus** *The defendant requests a sentence reduction.*

- Not all words with these endings are nominalizations, and not all nominalizations are "bad." However, if you see a word with one of these endings, stop to see if you can make your sentence shorter or stronger by using a base verb instead.

4. Avoid words that lead to vague or imprecise sentences
   - There are some "buzz" words to avoid. Words like "involve," "whether," or "the court considers" inevitably lead to a sentence that does not take a position.

> **EXAMPLE:** *Decisions on preliminary injunctions involve several factors* **versus** *A court considers four factors in deciding whether to impose a preliminary injunction.*

> **EXAMPLE: Wordy**
>
> *In determining whether a suspect comprehends the consequence of the Fifth Amendment waiver, the Supreme Court does not require that every consequence is <u>known by</u> the defendant, only that the waiver <u>is made</u> voluntarily, knowingly, and intelligently.*

> **EXAMPLE: Better**
>
> *The Supreme Court does not require that a suspect comprehend every possible consequence of the Fifth Amendment waiver, only that the waiver is voluntary, knowing, and intelligent.*

EXAMPLE: Wordy/Imprecise

A defendant who is arrested or charged with a crime is entitled to a speedy trial under the Sixth Amendment by taking into account such factors as delays and consequences to the defendant, as well as prejudice to the defendant.

EXAMPLE: Better

The Sixth Amendment guarantees a speedy trial for all criminal defendants; courts consider the length and reason for the delay and any prejudice to the defendant.

---

5. Use short sentences.
   - If your sentences are long, check for passive voice, nominalizations, or vague language.
   - Do a random spot check and count words in a sentence. Average length should be below 25 words.
   - If necessary, chop up thoughts into two or more sentences.

6. Use transitions
   - Transitional phrases are used to show relationships between an individual paragraph and the preceding and succeeding ones.
   - They are helpful to the reader because they provide clarity, structure, and development of the paper.
   - "Moreover," "likewise," and "on the other hand" are examples of transitional words.

7. Use Microsoft Word (or another built-in program) to fix passive voice, grammar, and style
   - Find passive voice by doing a word find for "be," "been," etc.
   - The search shows you where the word "be" leads to a passive construction.
   - Set your Word options to identify grammar and style problems (as well as spell check).

8. Use spell check but do not substitute grammar programs for your own proofing. Spell check will not always pick up a misspelled or incorrect word.

> **EXAMPLES OF SPELL CHECK ERRORS:** *The court reversed defendant's motion for a new trail; Defendant's <u>councilor</u> was present for the police line-up.*

9. There are many good grammar programs based on artificial intelligence, such as Grammarly, that you can use to check your spelling and grammar. These programs are effective and especially helpful if you have not had formal grammar training. Proofreading is still essential. Reading your text aloud is one way to catch mistakes. If you have time, take a break before proofreading so that you review the writing with fresh eyes.

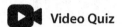 **Video Quiz**

CHAPTER 14

Legal Writing and ChatGPT

INTRODUCTION

Artificial intelligence (AI) has been integral to law practice for quite a while. Generative AI such as ChatGPT, Bard, Bing, and Lexis+ AI are just some of the examples of the generative AI programs that are relevant to legal practice. Here, we will focus on ChatGPT.

ChatGPT is an acronym for Generative Pre-Trained Transformer. As the name suggests, the program uses large language models mined from the Internet to predict the next word in a sentence. Humans use successive prompts to fine-tune output and give "better answers." Users can ask ChatGPT to write anything, including papers and essays, creative stories, policies and handbooks, and professional letters. Key for law students and lawyers, ChatGPT can also generate legal memos, legal analysis, client letters, and any number of documents relevant to law practice.

As of this textbook's writing, ChatGPT is quickly getting the attention of law professors, judges, and lawyers. The AI landscape is evolving so rapidly that any attempt to capture its relevance to law students will be obsolete almost immediately. Thus, what follows is a distillation of points that—today at least—law students should be familiar with when considering using ChatGPT.

LAW SCHOOL POLICIES ON CHATGPT

Many colleges and universities have policies that address the use of AI and ChatGPT. These policies range from a complete prohibition against using any form of AI to guidelines on how AI can be effectively and accurately used. Law professors, especially legal writing professors, will most likely have their own policies or guidelines for their students. Is it plagiarism to reprint the results of a well-honed ChatGPT prompt as part of an assignment? That question should be addressed to your professors, who may have policies banning ChatGPT use or requiring attribution if ChatGPT is used in an assignment.

RESEARCH

Law students, lawyers, and judges rely on AI-assisted legal research programs like Westlaw, Lexis, and Bloomberg. These established websites are reliable and widely used. ChatGPT as a tool in legal analysis is not yet sufficiently accurate. While ChatGPT can be prompted to write a full legal memo, complete with legal analysis and citations to cases, the law that ChatGPT cites may be entirely invented—the result of so-called "hallucinations" created by AI. For example, in *Mata v. Avianca, Inc.*, 2023 WL 3696209 *17 (S.D.N.Y. 2023), the court sanctioned a lawyer for submitting a legal memorandum that contained citations to invented legal authorities. The lawyer admitted he had used ChatGPT and did not check to verify the citations for accuracy. In May 2023, a federal judge in Texas posted a new rule specific to his court requiring a certificate that attests "either that no portion of the filing was drafted by generative artificial intelligence (such as ChatGPT, Harvey.AI, or Google Bard) or that any language drafted by generative artificial intelligence was checked for accuracy, using print reporters or traditional legal databases, by a human being." Judge Brantley Starr, *Mandatory Certification Regarding Generative Artificial Intelligence* (November 27, 2023), https://www.txnd.uscourts.gov/judge/judge-brantley-starr. While ChatGPT may be helpful in creating some types of text for legal writing, it will not (as of now) produce accurate legal authority.

Lexis+ has introduced a Generative AI function that utilizes its own databases to answer legal questions and draft documents. It is possible that Lexis+ AI will save lawyers time and money as it develops. As of this writing, the function does not yet choose the best law to answer a legal question, and the jury is still out whether Lexis+ AI can accurately and thoroughly apply the law to a client's facts. You should gather the facts from your client, and you must always evaluate any documents or analysis produced by Lexis+ AI, or other Generative AI, through your own expert reading of legal sources. In addition, always check with your school and/or employer, and consider your ethical obligations, before using Generative AI tools.

ETHICS

Using ChatGPT implicates a lawyer's ethical obligations in a number of ways. While law students, particularly first-year students, are not bound by the Professional Conduct Code, it's a good idea to be familiar with how using ChatGPT could conflict with a lawyer's ethical responsibilities. Lawyers are ethically bound to be up to date on legal technology, which means knowing what ChatGPT can and cannot do. If ChatGPT creates made-up legal authority, lawyers are bound to use the technology responsibly and with knowledge of its limitations. Lawyers are also bound by rules of confidentiality. This means that lawyers inputting client information to ChatGPT or other forms of AI must consider whether they may be disclosing confidential client information to the AI company. Ethical rules also prohibit the unauthorized practice of law. Lawyers can be assisted by nonlawyers (including nonhuman assistance), but they have a duty to supervise the work, and they are responsible for the work done.

These are some of the examples of how AI implicates a lawyer's ethical obligations. Given the speed at which AI is being integrated into the legal field, there will be more areas of concern, and, to date, many of the ethical issues have not been fully fleshed out.

BIAS

Output from ChatGPT is vulnerable to content that is biased. Because the program is generated by humans using natural language and large datasets of information and words mined from the Internet, there is a potential for outcomes to mimic human biases. Prejudice and potentially harmful stereotyping essentially become encoded in the process and consequently may be present in ChatGPT's output. Marginalized groups are particularly affected by such biases.[1] Users of AI for legal writing must exercise Generative AI literacy skills and heighten their awareness of potentially harmful bias that may be present in any AI output they rely on.

---

1. Celeste Kidd and Abeba Birhane, *How AI can distort human beliefs,* Science, June 2023, https://www.science.org/doi/10.1126/science.adi0248.

Examples of Different Types of Legal Writing

PREDICTIVE WRITING TO INTERPRET: WRITING ABOUT LAW (NOT RELATED TO A CLIENT'S FACTS)

Predictive legal writing can take other forms. For instance, you may be asked to interpret a statute or explain a new case that has just come down. A predictive memorandum could also be used to prepare for a settlement negotiation or a decision not to file a complaint. Or, you may be asked to explain a statute or legal principle. For example, imagine that the firm or business where you are working has several clients who are landlords. A new version of a tenant eviction process has just been enacted. You have been asked to interpret the steps necessary to evict a tenant under the statute.

Starting on the next page is an example of what your response would look like.

MEMORANDUM

To: Supervisor
From: Student Lawyer
Date: August 2, 20XX
Re: New Hampshire Eviction Process

Question:
What steps are required to initiate and carry out eviction proceedings for a tenant who has not paid rent?

Summary of Relevant Law:
The eviction process in NH is a multi-step process set out in N.H. Rev. Stat. Ann. §540 and District Court Rule 5. First, the landlord must make a demand for rent. If no rent is paid then the landlord can file a Notice to Quit. The tenant is entitled to a hearing to challenge the demand. At the hearing, if the landlord sustains a claim of unpaid rent, the judge can order the tenant to pay back rent and a writ of possession that authorizes a sheriff to remove the tenant from the premises.

Steps to Evict a Tenant:

1. Demand for Rent
First, the landlord must make a demand for rent from the tenant. N.H. Rev. Stat. Ann. §540:3-4. The demand must state the amount owed and it must be served on the tenant personally or left at the residence. Either way, the landlord must show proof of the service by an attested copy of the demand and an affidavit that sets out that service was made. N.H. Rev. Stat. Ann. §540:5. The district court clerk's office has the forms needed; however, the landlord is not required to use the forms. N.H. Rev. Stat. Ann. §540:5.

2. Notice to Quit
The landlord must also provide the tenant with a written Notice to Quit (also called an "eviction notice"). N.H. Rev. Stat. Ann. §540:2(I). This can be done at the same time as the demand for rent. The Notice must be in writing and must state the specific reason for the eviction. N.H. Rev. Stat. Ann. §540:3(I-III)). When the reason for termination of tenancy is nonpayment of rent, 30 days' notice of eviction is sufficient. N.H. Rev. Stat. Ann. §540:3(II). The Notice to Quit must also inform the tenant that the tenant can avoid eviction by paying the past rent plus $15 in liquidated damages. N.H. Rev. Stat. Ann. §540:3(II), (III); 540:9.

3. Service of the Notice to Quit

The landlord can either serve the Notice to Quit personally with the tenant, or leave it at the tenant's residence. NH. Rev. Stat. Ann. §540:5. Like the rule for the demand of rent, the landlord must show proof of the service by an attested copy of the Notice and an affidavit that sets out that service was made. The district court clerk's office has the forms needed. The landlord is not required to use the forms so long as all the information is on the notice. N.H. Rev. Stat. Ann. §540:5.

4. Writ of Summons

If the tenant has not complied with the demand for rent or the Notice to Quit, the landlord can go to the district court clerk's office and ask that the court issue a Writ of Summons. N.H. Rev. Stat. Ann. §540:13. Once the Writ is issued, a sheriff will serve the Writ and the tenant will have seven days to either leave the premises or request a hearing by filing an appearance at the district court. N.H. Rev. Stat. Ann. §540:13(II)(d)(1).

5. The Court Hearing

If the tenant requests a hearing, the court will schedule one within ten days after the date of the tenant's appearance is filed. N.H. Rev. Stat. Ann. §540:13(V). Both the tenant and the landlord are entitled to discovery prior to the hearing pursuant to N.H. Dist. Ct. R. 5.6. N.H. Rev. Stat. Ann. §540:13 (IV). At the hearing, the landlord would present the case for the unpaid rent and show proof of the demand and Notice to Quit. The tenant is allowed to present evidence in defense. N.H. Rev. Stat. Ann. §540:13(III). The court will decide the matter and can award the landlord the unpaid rent up to $1,500.

If the tenant does not file an appearance, the court will send a notice of default to the tenant within three days of issuing a Writ of Possession. N.H. Rev. Stat. Ann. §540:14(I). Once the Writ of Possession is issued the sheriff is authorized to remove the tenant from the premises.

Notice that this memorandum is purely about law. There is no application of the law to a client's problem.

Predictive writing is typically done "in house," meaning that it is done for internal use. In other words, it is done within a law office or by a clerk in a judge's chambers. Because this type of legal writing is done to inform and educate and not to persuade, there is little likelihood of writing an objective analysis in a brief for a court. That is where persuasive legal writing comes in.

PERSUASIVE WRITING: THE PERSUASIVE MEMORANDUM OR BRIEF

Now imagine that you have completed your first year of law school and are working in a state prosecutor's office. You are asked to draft a persuasive motion *in limine* arguing that the prior evidence regarding Albert's (the example from Chapter 2) removal of the turkey from the supermarket should be admissible in a trial against her for the theft of the ham.

The format and content of persuasive legal writing is similar to objective writing. However, instead of informing the reader, the task is to *convince* the reader that whatever position you want the court to take is supported and thus should prevail. The tone (language) used will be slightly different. In the example starting on the next page, notice how similar the structure and content of the memorandum is to the predictive memorandum.

STATE OF NEW HAMPSHIRE
MERRIMACK, SS.
SEPTEMBER TERM 2013
SUPERIOR COURT

State of New Hampshire
v.
Maureen Albert
No. 000-2013-CV-0000

STATE'S MOTION *IN LIMINE* TO ADMIT EVIDENCE OF OTHER BAD ACTS

NOW COMES the State of New Hampshire, by and through its attorney, Leslie Witman of the Office of the State Prosecutor, and hereby seeks an order from this Court admitting evidence to trial regarding Defendant Maureen Albert's (hereinafter "Albert" or "Defendant") prior bad act of shoplifting a turkey from a Hannaford Supermarket.

INTRODUCTION

Defendant's prior bad act of shoplifting is admissible under New Hampshire Rule of Evidence 404(b) because it is relevant to show Defendant's intent, not mere character evidence; there is clear proof that the Defendant actually committed the act; and the probative value of the evidence outweighs any prejudicial impact on a jury. As previously stipulated, this motion addresses only the first question of relevance.

Defendant is currently charged with theft of a ham from a Hannaford Supermarket in Concord, New Hampshire in February 20XX, just three months after a similar incident in which Defendant shoplifted a turkey from the same store. By claiming that she did not intend to steal the ham for which she is currently charged, Defendant put her own intent at issue. As such, Defendant's similar prior act is relevant to her state of mind at the time of the second shoplifting incident and ought to be admissible to rebut her claim that she stole the meat by mere accident.

In further support of its motion to admit this evidence at trial, the State says as follows:

BACKGROUND

Ms. Maureen Albert removed a turkey placed in the bottom of her shopping cart without paying from the Hannaford's Supermarket in Concord, New Hampshire in November 2011. Albert returned the turkey after being confronted, was warned about her behavior, and was not prosecuted. Just three months later, in February 20XX, Albert shoplifted a spiral ham using a shopping cart from the same store. When confronted by an employee in the parking lot, Albert stated that she left the store because she had forgotten her wallet in her car. She brought her state of mind into issue even further by also stating that she did not intend to steal the ham and had removed it from the store accidentally. The State has now charged Albert with shoplifting for the second offense.

ARGUMENT

Ms. Maureen Albert's prior act of taking a turkey from the Concord, New Hampshire Hannaford's without paying is relevant to prove that she intended to shoplift the ham for which she is currently charged from the same store. When evidence has a direct bearing on an issue actually in dispute, and a clear and logical connection exists between that act and the crime charge, then the evidence is relevant for a purpose other than character. *McGlew*, 658 A.2d 1191, 1194. Albert's prior act is relevant to refute her claim that she took the ham accidentally. In addition, the prior act is factually similar and close in time because she removed meat without paying twice in three months from the same store.

1. Direct Bearing on Issue in Dispute

Albert's prior act of taking a turkey is relevant to refute her claim that shoplifting the ham was by accident. Generally, evidence of a prior act is relevant to refute a defendant's claim that the crime was committed by accident. *Lesnick*, 677 A.2d 686, 690 (N.H. 1996). For example, in *Lesnick*, where the defendant claimed she stabbed her husband in self-defense because she believed him to be an unknown intruder, the court admitted evidence of a prior act because it was relevant to show that absence of an accident. *Id*. In contrast, when a defendant denies any involvement in a crime, prior act evidence is excluded. *State v. Blackey*, 623 A.2d 1333, 1334 (N.H. 1993). By denying the crime altogether, the defendant in *Blackey* had not placed her intent or propensity at issue, so the prior act evidence was not relevant and the court excluded it. *Id*.

Albert's prior act is relevant because she claimed that she took the ham by accident. Similar to the defendant in *Lesnick*, who admitted to stabbing her husband but claimed it was by accident, Albert made her intent an issue by claiming she took the ham unintentionally when returning to her car. Evidence of her prior similar act is relevant to rebut Albert's claim of taking the ham by accident. Because the evidence of the prior removal of meat is not offered to show Albert's character or propensity, but rather to rebut her claim of mere mistake, it is admissible.

2. Clear and Logical Connection

Albert's prior act is also relevant because a clear, logical connection exists between the charged act of shoplifting a ham and the prior act of taking a turkey from the same store within three months of each other. Where the acts are factually similar, and the prior act is "not so remote in time as to eliminate the nexus" between the prior act and the crime charged, then a clear, logical connection exists. *McGlew*, 658 A.2d at 1194. Where a precise chain of reasoning between the prior act and the charged act exists, the prior evidence is admissible. *Id.* at 1195. In *Lesnick*, a logical connection existed between the prior stabbing and the charged stabbing because the defendant committed each crime under similar emotional circumstances against the same victim using the same weapon. *Id.* The factual similarities between the two acts concluded that the defendant intended the second act since two identical "accidents" within a few months of each other were unlikely. *Id.*

Albert's prior act and current charge are so significantly similar that a clear and logical nexus connects the two events. In *McGlew*, where a prior accusation of sexual molestation and the charged act of sexual assault, which occurred six years later, involved a different victim of different age and gender and a different sex act, the prior charge was inadmissible because there was not a sufficient nexus between the two acts. 658 A.2d at 1194. The factual differences could not permit the conclusion that the defendant had the same intent during each act and therefore the prior act was inadmissible. *Id.*

The virtually identical facts of Albert's two acts permit the conclusion that she intended the second act since two identical "accidents" within such a short time frame is unlikely. The turkey and ham were similar products removed from the same store, using thesame method of removal—suggesting that the second shoplifting incident was intentional. Similar to the facts in *Lesnick*, where the close similarity of the two acts rendered the prior act relevant to the defendant's intent in stabbing her husband, here the virtually identical circumstances and facts permit the conclusion that Albert's prior act is also relevant to her intent to steal the ham.

In addition to the factual similarities of Albert's two acts, the time frame between the two shoplifting incidents further indicates that her intent was to steal the ham. When two acts are close in proximity, the more likely an actor had the same intent at both times. *See Lesnick*, 677 A.2d at 690 (emphasizing the temporal proximity of the charged act and the prior act). In *Lesnick*, the prior act was relevant because it occurred only two months before the charged crime, whereas in *McGlew*, the prior act committed six years earlier was not admitted. 677 A.2d at 690; 658 A.2d at 1194. Albert's prior removal of a ham and subsequent shoplifting of a turkey just three months later is similar to Lesnick, who committed the two acts within two months. Although a person may make one mistake, she is unlikely to make two nearly identical mistakes within such a short time. The close proximity in time between Albert's two acts further supports their logical connection and renders her prior act of shoplifting relevant. Because the prior act demonstrates Albert's intent, and is not mere character or propensity evidence, it is relevant to the current charge.

Albert's argument that allowing the bad act evidence against her goes against the purpose behind 404(b) and its limitations is without merit. The concern that a defendant not be convicted on the basis of character is met where, as here, there is a sufficient, specific purpose for its admission. By claiming that she mistakenly took the turkey, Albert has placed her own intent to commit theft at issue. Thus, the purpose of the evidence is to refute Albert's claim of accident, and not to demonstrate her bad character.

WHEREFORE the State of New Hampshire respectfully requests that this Honorable Court:

A. Find that evidence of Defendant's prior act of taking a turkey from the Concord, New Hampshire Hannaford's in November 2011 is admissible at Albert's trial; and

B. Grant such other and further relief as this Court deems just and proper.

Respectfully submitted,
THE STATE OF NEW HAMPSHIRE
By its attorney,
Date: September 22, 2013   By: /s/ Leslie Witman
Leslie Witman
NH Bar # 000
Assistant County Attorney
County Prosecutors Bureau
3 Main Street
Concord, NH 03301

CERTIFICATE OF SERVICE

I hereby certify on this 22nd day of September 2013, copies of the foregoing Motion *In Limine* were sent by e-mail to Maureen Albert and her counsel.

/s/ Leslie Witman, Esq
Leslie Witman, Esq

WRITING TO A CLIENT: COMMUNICATING TO A LAYPERSON

Communicating with clients makes up a lot of what lawyers do. Typically, lawyers write to clients to keep them updated and to explain to them the legal, practical, and procedural ramifications of their cases. Client letters (which are often done in e-mails) can also memorialize decisions that clients have made, such as to settle a case or proceed to court. In addition, client letters may address whether a client wants to agree to a contract term.

While some clients will be lawyers, most legal correspondence is between a lawyer and a non-lawyer. This book, and most legal writing instruction, will demand that you always write in plain English. However, the need for clarity is especially critical when writing to a client.

On the next page is an example of a client letter that Albert's lawyer might send her regarding whether she should plead guilty to a reduced sentence and avoid a trial. Notice the absence of specific references to cases. Notice that this memorandum is purely about law. There is no application of the law to a client's problem.

Maureen Albert
3 Pike Street
Concord, New Hampshire

Re: Shoplifting case

Dear Ms. Albert:

As requested, I am writing to give you my opinion on whether you should accept the prosecutor's offer of a misdemeanor plea and a probationary sentence. As you and I discussed, the key question is whether your prior incident at the same Hannaford will come into the trial as evidence. If the judge allows the evidence, the likelihood of a not guilty verdict diminishes. This letter will address why the prior incident will likely be allowed into evidence.

Explanation of Relevant Law

As I explained to you at our meeting, evidence of prior similar activity is allowed to come into a trial under certain limited circumstances. The prior incident must be relevant for a purpose other than just to show character. In other words, the prior incident must have a direct bearing on the current case and there must be a clear, logical connection between the prior incident and the current case. Thus, the judge can allow prior evidence of similar conduct if the prosecutor can prove that the evidence is relevant and that there is a logical reason to do so.

Your Case

The prosecutor will argue that the incident involving the ham should be allowed at your trial because it involves very similar conduct and it shows that you didn't take the turkey by accident. In your trial, the prosecutor will have to prove that you had an intent to steal the turkey. She will argue that, by claiming that the turkey removal was an accident, you have put your intent at issue, which, she will say, opens the door for her to put in evidence of the ham incident. She will argue that your claim of accident can be refuted because you did a similar act recently. In addition, she will argue that the two scenarios are so similar and close in time that you could not have removed the turkey by accident.

I think that there is a good chance that the judge will allow evidence of your prior incident to come into the trial. Because the acts are so similar and close in time, the judge will probably find that the jury can use the evidence as proof that you did not take the turkey by accident. We will argue that this evidence would unfairly prejudice the jury against you and there is law we can use to support this argument. However, my belief is that the judge will not rule in our favor.

Conclusion and Next Steps

The prosecutor has offered one year of probation in exchange for your guilty plea to the theft. Whether to accept this offer is entirely up to you. If you decide to reject the offer, I will do my best to represent you at trial. It can be hard to predict what a jury will do. However, given the likelihood that the judge will allow the prior incident to come into evidence, I think it will be difficult, though not impossible, to get a not guilty verdict. If you were to go to trial, the judge could give you a longer probationary sentence, deferred jail time, or actual jail time (though I think this is unlikely). Given what you have told me about your need to care for your family and your desire to put this incident behind you, I would advise that you accept the prosecutor's offer. I am happy to discuss this further. I know it is a big decision and you want to feel as though you are making the right choice for you.

Please call my office and set up a time to go over this information and any questions you have.

Sincerely,
Lawyer.

There are, of course, many other kinds of writing that you will do: drafting legislation, making notes to a file, writing judicial opinions (if you are a judicial law clerk or become a judge), writing contracts and legal documents, and perhaps writing scholarly pieces. And in law school (and on the bar exam), you will be writing exam answers. The skills you learn in your legal writing class will help you be an effective writer in all of these situations.

Additional Example of a Predictive Legal Memorandum

On the next page is an additional example of a predictive memo. Notice how the synthesized rule in the first paragraph of the Discussion indicates three parts to the relevant law on a child's contributory negligence. The focus sentences of the following three rule explanation paragraphs signal which part is being addressed in the paragraph, using similar language so that the reader easily follows the analysis. The three rule application paragraphs also use focus sentences to signal to the reader which part of the rule is being applied.

MEMORANDUM

To: Professor
From: Student
Date: November 8, XXXX
Re: Murphy Jackland Negligence Action

Issue

Under Texas law, which holds a minor to a lesser standard of care than an adult, was Murphy Jackland, a 14-year-old with disabilities, contributorily negligent when she was struck by Susan Green's car as she walked to her school bus stop wearing dark clothing without a light?

Summary

Probably not. Texas courts measure a minor's standard of care by comparing it to the care that a child of the same age, intelligence, experience, and capacity would use. For a court to hold Murphy contributorily negligent, it would have to find that she failed to meet this standard of care. Because of her mental challenges, a court would evaluate Murphy by the standard of an ordinary 10-year-old and determine that a child of this age could not have foreseen the danger posed by the weather and road conditions. Thus, the court would likely find that Murphy's failure to wear bright clothing or carry a light was reasonable and not contributorily negligent given her developmental age.

Facts

Our client, Murphy Jackland, suffered a serious injury after a car driven by Susan Green hit her as she walked to her bus stop. Murphy is a 14-year-old girl who is mentally and behaviorally four years behind others her age. Murphy wants to sue Green for negligence. We must determine if Green is likely to succeed with an affirmative defense of contributory negligence.

Murphy lives with her family near the bottom of Wagon Hill Road in Brownville. Murphy's morning trip to the school bus had followed the same daily route for three years. Murphy would walk down her driveway and turn right. She would stay on the right-hand side of the road until she got to the top of the hill. At the top, she would check for traffic in both directions, cross to the left side of the street, and walk the rest of the way to her bus stop.

Last December 6, just after her 14th birthday, Murphy left the house to go to the school bus as usual. She had not quite reached the top of the hill when Green's car hit her. It was early morning, dark, and the road was snow-covered with snowbanks along the shoulders. There were no sidewalks. Murphy was wearing dark clothing and was not carrying a light.

Green was driving in the same direction on Wagon Hill Road at a modest speed. As another vehicle approached, Green dimmed her headlights. When she re-engaged her bright lights, she saw Murphy in the road. Green hit Murphy, causing her to suffer internal injuries and broken bones.

Discussion

A judge would probably not find Murphy contributorily negligent because she acted with due care under the minor standard. A child between ages 5 and 14 may be contributorily negligent if the child fails to use such care as would be reasonable for a child of the same age, intelligence, experience, and capacity under the same or similar circumstances. *Rudes v. Gottschalk*, 324 S.W.2d 201, 206 (Tex. 1959); *MacConnell v. Hill*, 569 S.W.2d 524, 527 (Tex. App. 1978); *City of Austin v. Hoffman*, 379 S.W.2d 103, 107 (Tex. App. 1964); *Dallas Ry. & Terminal Co. v. Rogers*, 218 S.W.2d 456, 458 (Tex. 1949). A child's developmental capacity is relevant in assessing the correct standard of care. *Soledad v. Lara*, 762 S.W.2d 212, 214 (Tex. App. 1988). Texas courts are reluctant to hold children responsible even if they fail to keep a proper lookout or heed warnings. *MacConnell*, 569 S.W.2d at 527. The test of negligence is different for children than adults because children's powers and abilities to anticipate danger and harmful consequences are often not the same as adults. *Rudes*, 324 S.W.2d at 206.

The standard of care applied to a child is measured by the behavior that would be reasonable under the circumstances given the child's particular abilities. *Houston & T.C.R. Co. v. Bulger*, 80 S.W. 557, 561 (Tex. App. 1904); *Soledad v. Lara*, 762 S.W.2d 212, 214 (Tex. App. 1988). In *Bulger*, a 13-year-old boy with a low mental capacity scalded both legs when hot water and steam escaped a boiler at a railroad company's pumping station. 80 S.W. at 561. The court upheld the lower court's jury charge to consider the boy's low mental capacity, holding that the boy may not have had the same discretion that could reasonably be expected from other 13-year-old children. *Id.* Similarly, in *Soledad*, a 16-year-old boy sued the design engineers of a drainage ditch where he was injured while playing. 762 S.W.2d at 214. The boy sued under the attractive nuisance doctrine, and the court held that even though ordinarily the attractive nuisance doctrine does not apply to children over 14, it did apply in Soledad's case because the boy was lacking in mental development, as evidenced by his attendance in special education classes. *Id.*

Texas courts are reluctant to find children contributorily negligent where they have failed to keep a proper lookout for their safety or to heed warnings. *See Guzman v. Guajardo*, 761 S.W.2d 506, 510 (Tex. App. 1988); *MacConnell*, 569 S.W.2d at 527. In *Guzman*, a seven-year-old boy was hit and killed by a car as he crossed a road. 761 S.W.2d at 510. The court upheld the lower court's decision that the boy was not contributorily negligent even though he was warned by his mother and grandmother specifically to stay off that particular road earlier that day. *Id.* Similarly, in *MacConnell*, a six-year-old boy was sprayed with hot steam and water when the defendant negligently removed the end of a car's radiator hose without first properly releasing the pressure. 569 S.W.2d at 525. The defendant had warned the boy twice to move away from the car. *Id.* The court reversed the lower court's jury decision that found the boy contributorily negligent, noting that his failure to keep a proper lookout was insufficient to bar his recovery because of his inferior ability to foresee and anticipate danger. *Id* at 528.

The experience and education of a child in the injury-causing activity does not necessarily make a child contributorily negligent. *Dallas Ry. & Terminal Co.*, 218 S.W.2d at 461; *Guzman*, 761 S.W.2d at 510. In *Dallas Ry. & Terminal Co.*, an 11-year-old girl familiar with the traffic hazards of downtown Dallas, was hit by a bus as she crossed an intersection. 218 S.W.2d at 461. Reversing the jury's findings that the girl was contributorily negligent for failing to keep a proper lookout, the court held that even if a child has been instructed and is experienced in traffic matters, a higher standard of care should not be applied because the child is still subject to the reckless and impulsive nature of youth. *Id.* Similarly, the boy in *Guzman* was educated by his mother in traffic matters and was taught the importance of keeping a lookout for cars. *Guzman*, 761 S.W.2d at 510. The boy's traffic education did not affect the court's decision against finding him contributorily negligent. *Id.*

In evaluating Murphy's potential contributory negligence, a court would first examine what behavior was reasonable given her age and mental capacity. Like the minors in *Bulger* and *Soledad*, who both showed signs of mental challenges, here testing has revealed that Murphy is mentally and behaviorally four years behind other children her age. Although Murphy was 14 years old at the time of the accident, the court will likely apply the standard of care of a ten-year-old child. Moreover, as in *Bulger*, where the court instructed the jury to consider that the child may not have had the same discretion that could be reasonably expected from other children of the same age, here, the court is likely to give a jury the same instruction regarding Murphy's developmental age.

A court would also probably determine that Murphy's failure to keep a proper lookout at her age and mental capacity could not have foreseen the danger surrounding the circumstances on the day of the accident. Unlike *Guzman*, where the child's mother had instructed him in traffic safety, our facts do not indicate that Murphy was warned about the hazards of walking to the bus stop on a dark, snowy street. Even if Murphy had been warned of the danger on her road, it is unlikely that this would affect the court's decision in her favor, given that the warnings made no difference to the standard of care in Guzman. A court may determine that Murphy's neglect to wear reflective clothing and to carry a light was a failure to keep a proper lookout for her safety. However, like the boy in *MacConnell*, Murphy's inferior ability to anticipate danger as a minor should protect her from being held contributorily negligent. Her case may even be stronger than *MacConnell* because, arguably, she kept a proper lookout by walking on the right side of the street to the top of the hill until she could safely cross, thus avoiding the problem of non-visible oncoming traffic.

Murphy's experience walking the same route for three years does not make it more likely that a court will find her contributorily negligent. Like the girl in *Dallas Ry. & Terminal Co.*, Murphy was experienced in the everyday hazards presented by her route. Her manner of walking to the top of the hill before crossing the street shows her awareness of traffic dangers. However, the girl's experience with traffic in *Dallas Ry. & Terminal Co.* did not make her contributorily negligent because her relative youth still could have lowered her ability to judge the circumstances. Similarly, Murphy's experience with traffic should not increase the chance that a court will find her contributorily negligent.

Conclusion

A court will probably consider Murphy's disabilities and her mental capacity. Any evidence of Murphy's experience in traffic matters, or her failure to keep a proper lookout or to heed warnings, is unlikely to result in a finding that permits Green to raise the affirmative defense of contributory negligence.

Case Brief for *Winstead*

State v. Winstead, 150 M.G. 244 (2003).

Parties: State of New Hampshire (prosecutor) and William T. Winstead (defendant)

Procedural History: Defendant found guilty at bench trial in Claremont District Court. Appealed directly to the Magnolia Supreme Court.

Facts: Police found defendant "sleeping upright" in the driver's seat of his car in a Wal-Mart parking lot. Engine was on. He testified at trial that he couldn't drive so he got in the car and ran the engine to stay warm. He testified that although he had no intention of driving, he unlocked the door, sat in the driver's seat, pushed in the clutch, selected neutral, started engine, and turned on the heater. Defendant admitted to consuming a 6 pack and failed field sobriety tests. At the station, defendant produced a BAC of .07 on the breathalyzer. His blood test came back with a .08.

Issue: Whether (1) the court erred in admitting the blood test, (2) the defendant's equal protection rights were violated because of police testimony that he does not usually disturb people sleeping in RVs in the parking lot, and (3) there was insufficient evidence to find that the defendant was in control of his vehicle.

Holding: (1) the blood test issue was not preserved for appeal. (2) The defendant's equal protection rights were not violated. (3) Yes, there was sufficient evidence to show that the defendant was in actual physical control of his vehicle.

Rule with respect to 3rd issue, the issue relevant to our sample case: People will have actual physical control over their vehicle if they start the car from the driver's seat before they fall asleep. (248)

Reasoning: Starting the car is "as close as possible" to driving it.

Disposition: Lower court decision affirmed.

Case Brief for *O'Malley*

State v. O'Malley, 120 M.G. 507 (2002).

Parties: State of New Hampshire (prosecutor) and John T. O'Malley (defendant)

Procedural History: Defendant was found guilty by the "Trial Court" of DUI, 2nd offense and operating a motor vehicle with a revoked license. (508)

Facts: Police found the defendant in a parked car on a public way in front of Arthur Lambro's house. The defendant was "slumped over," eyes closed in the driver's seat with the keys in the ignition and the engine off. Police knocked on the window but did not awaken the defendant until they opened the car door. Once awakened, the defendant "pushed in the clutch and tried to shift the gear." Police asked the defendant to get out of the car and upon learning he had no license, helped him to the police cruiser. The defendant "stumbled, staggered, and nearly fell." Empty and full beer bottles found in the car. At trial, the defendant testified that he had hitchhiked to Arthur Lambro's house. Later in the evening, Lambro asked the defendant to warm up the car and then he would drive him home, but the defendant instead fell asleep.

Issue: Whether the trial court erred in finding that the defendant was in actual physical control of the vehicle. (509)

Holding: Yes, the trial court erred.

Rule: Mere presence in the car is not enough; to have actual physical control, there must be circumstantial evidence that the defendant drove or would imminently drive.

Reasoning: Defendant's account of what happened was "not unreasonable." Defendant's statement that he was warming up the car was sufficient circumstantial evidence.

Disposition: The Trial Court decision was reversed.

This is the completed chart from Chapter 7.

	Winstead	Holloran	O'Malley	Client facts
Decisive facts	D found asleep in the driver's seat of a car in a parking lot Engine running Before falling asleep, D unlocked door, sat in driver's seat, pushed clutch in, moved gear shift to neutral, started engine, and turned-on heater	D awake, sitting in driver's seat of truck parked legally, waiting for call from wife to pick her up from a party Engine off & lights off Keys in ignition	D had no intent to operate and did not operate vehicle D went out to friend's vehicle to start it so friend could give him a ride home D fell asleep in vehicle D found asleep in driver's seat Keys in ignition & engine off	**Decisive facts in Mr. Clover's case that relate to indicia of control** asleep in driver's seat key fob in his pocket turned on heat lights on decided not to call an Uber and instead to "sleep it off" in the car said could move car if parking space owner returned
Holding	D driving	D driving	D not driving	

Magnolia Cases on Defintion of "Way"
City of Aspen v. Peete
State v. Krause

224 M.G. 158
Supreme Court of Magnolia.

CITY OF ASPEN, Plaintiff and Respondent,
v.
Raymond K. PEETE, Defendant and Appellant.
No. 86–303.
Submitted Sept. 18, 1986.
Decided Nov. 24, 1986.
Rehearing Denied Jan. 13, 1987.

Synopsis

Defendant was convicted of driving while under the influence by the Aspen City Court, and he appealed. The Thirteenth Judicial District Court, Yellowstone County, G. Todd Baugh, J., denied defendant's motion to dismiss, and defendant again appealed. The Supreme Court, Morrison, J., held that motorist was operating vehicle "upon the ways of the state open to the public" for purpose of DUI statute, though motorist was exiting from private parking facility via up ramp at time of collision.

Affirmed.

Attorneys and Law Firms

**1268 *158 Sandall, Cavan, Smith, Howard & Grubbs, John J. Cavan, Aspen, for defendant and appellant.

Bonnie Sutherland, City Attorney's Office, Aspen, for plaintiff and respondent.

Opinion

MORRISON, Justice.

Raymond K. Peete, defendant, was convicted in Aspen City *159 Court of violating § 265-A:2, driving while under the influence of alcohol. He appealed his conviction to Yellowstone County District Court. Defendant filed a motion to dismiss, alleging that he was not operating a motor vehicle "upon the ways of the state open to the public," as required by the statute. The motion to dismiss was denied. Defendant was again convicted of violating § 265-A:2. Defendant appeals the District Court's failure to grant his motion to dismiss. We affirm.

**1269 Defendant's motion to dismiss was accompanied by a stipulation of facts. The following facts are taken from that stipulation:

Defendant was arrested at approximately 10:30 p.m., August 2, 1984, in the Northern Hotel parking garage for driving while under the influence of alcohol.

The parking garage is a privately owned and operated facility. It consists of five levels of parking spaces. The spaces on the ground level and the below-ground level are rented on a monthly basis. The top three levels are available to the general public for an hourly fee. After 5:00 p.m., the general public may also use unoccupied spaces on the two lower levels.

Use of the garage is controlled by employees of the owner of the garage. The parking attendant occupies a ticket booth located between the entry and exit lanes of the facility. Patrons entering the garage receive a ticket from the attendant who is stationed at the ticket booth. Upon exiting the parking facility, the patron must stop at the ticket booth, show the attendant his ticket and pay the appropriate fee. All patrons use the same entry and exit. However, monthly renters need not stop at the booth.

Defendant rents a parking space on the below-ground level. On the night he was arrested, defendant was exiting the lowest level via an up-ramp when his vehicle collided with a motorcycle parked in an area near the ramp reserved for bicycles and motorcycles. Defendant advised the parking attendant of the accident and was subsequently arrested.

The sole issue raised on appeal is:

Did defendant, Raymond Peete, operate a motor vehicle "upon the ways of the state open to the public", within the meaning of § 265-A:2, when he operated his vehicle within a privately owned and operated parking garage in Aspen, Magnolia?

The statute under which defendant was charged, § 265-A:2 states:

Persons under the influence of alcohol or drugs. (1) It is unlawful *160 and punishable as provided in 265-A:18 for any person who is under the influence of:

(a) alcohol to drive or be in actual physical control of a vehicle upon the ways of this state open to the public.

"Ways of this state open to the public" is defined at § 265-A:1, as "any highway, road, alley, lane, or other public or private place adapted and fitted for public travel that is in common use by the public."

Defendant contends that the Northern Hotel's parking garage is neither "adapted and fitted for public travel" nor "in common use by the public" because there is only one way to access the facility, access is achieved only upon obtaining a ticket from the parking attendant and use of the facility requires payment of a monthly or hourly fee. The City of Aspen contends that the garage is "adapted and fitted for public travel that

is in common use by the public" because the general public is permitted to use the facility for a small fee.

Section 265-A:2, was enacted in its present form by the 1983 Magnolia legislature. Because the language defining "the ways of this state open to the public" is less than clear, especially the term "in common use by the public", we turn to the legislative history to determine what the legislature had in mind.

Our statute is patterned after a City of Willow traffic ordinance, Willow Traffic Code §§ 11.12.1020 and 11.14.715.

. . . any road, alley, lane, parking area or any place, private or otherwise, adapted to and fitted for travel, that is in common use by the public.

**1270 When the House Judiciary Committee was debating the language of the original statute, Chairman Brown questioned whether "the language 'in common use by the public' would imply that a private bar parking lot, etc. would not be affected", Representative Keyser claimed that the whole phrase "fitted for public travel that is in common use by the public", would cover private parking lots. House Judiciary Committee Minutes, March 22, 1983, p. 16. Granted, a legislator's thoughts on what a statute means are not binding on this Court. However, from the discussion had in both the House and Senate Judiciary Committees with respect to this statute, it is clear that the statute was intended to include the operation of a motor vehicle within a private parking lot, as long as that lot is fitted for public travel and in common use by the public. The Northern Hotel's parking garage fits the definition.

This decision is consistent with Dogwood court opinions interpreting the City of Willow's traffic ordinance.

In *City of Willow v. Wright* (1967), 72 D.W.2d 556, 433 A.2d 906, defendant was arrested for driving, while intoxicated, upon an improved, 25 foot wide, hard-surface road owned by the Union Pacific Railroad. One of the four entries onto the two-block road was posted "Private Thoroughfare—10 M.P.H." However, local residents parked along the sides and used the road to access their homes. Commercial vehicles also regularly used the road. The Dogwood Supreme Court found the road to be a "road . . . adapted to and fitted for travel, that is in common use by the public with the consent, express or implied, of the owner . . . " because its surface was similar to nearby public thoroughfares and because the only restriction on travel imposed by the owner was a ten mile per hour speed limit.

The parking garage is paved. Driving areas are ***161** clearly indicated and the only restriction on travel imposed by the owner is that of the payment of a fee.

City of Willow v. Tolliver (1982), 31 D.W. App. 299, 641 A.2d 719, concerned an individual charged with operating a vehicle, while intoxicated, upon a private parking lot located at a major intersection. The parking lot was held by the court to be an area covered by the traffic ordinance because of its easy access to adjoining streets and its history of use by the public frequenting two taverns.

Similarly, the Northern Hotel's parking garage not only has a history of use by the public, the public is encouraged to use the facility. The facility is obviously fitted for public travel and in common use by the ****1271** public. It is thus covered by §§ 265-A:1 and 265-A:2.

Defendant's conviction is affirmed.

TURNAGE, C.J., and HARRISON, HUNT and GULBRANDSON, JJ., concur.

All Citations 224 M.G. 158, 729 A.2d 1268

403 M.G. 106
Supreme Court of Magnolia.

STATE of Magnolia, Plaintiff and Appellee,
v.
Clinton Scott KRAUSE, Defendant and Appellant.
DA 19-0042
Submitted on Briefs: December 9, 2020
Decided: February 2, 2021

Synopsis

Background: Defendant was convicted in the District Court of the Eighth Judicial District, County of Cascade, John W. Parker, J., of driving under the influence of alcohol (DUI), 4th or subsequent offense, and he appealed.

Holdings: The Supreme Court, McKinnon, J., held that:

there was legally sufficient evidence for jury to conclude that defendant was in a vehicle "on a way of this state open to the public," as that phrase was used in DUI statute.

Affirmed.

Baker, J., dissented and filed opinion in which Shea, J., joined.

*106 **224 APPEAL FROM: District Court of the Eighth Judicial District, In and For the County of Cascade, Cause No. DDC 17-586, Honorable John W. Parker, Presiding Judge

Attorneys and Law Firms

For Appellant: Chad Wright, Appellate Defender, Kristina L. Neal, Assistant Appellate Defender, Helena, Magnolia

For Appellee: Austin Knudsen, Magnolia Attorney General, Tammy K. Plubell, Assistant Attorney General, Helena, Magnolia, Joshua A. Racki, Cascade County Attorney, Jennifer L. Quick, Deputy County Attorney, Great Falls, Magnolia

Opinion

Justice Laurie McKinnon delivered the Opinion of the Court.

*107 Appellant, Clinton Scott Krause, appeals his conviction entered in the Eighth Judicial District Court, Cascade County. A jury convicted Krause of Driving Under the Influence of Alcohol (DUI), 4th or subsequent offense, after the District Court denied Krause's motion to dismiss and motion for mistrial. We affirm and address the following issue on appeal:

> Whether the District Court abused its discretion when it denied Krause's motion to dismiss for insufficient evidence.

FACTUAL AND PROCEDURAL BACKGROUND

On September 27, 2017, at about 9:40 p.m., Officer Meek of the Great Falls Police Department was dispatched to the area of 6th Avenue South and Chowen Springs Loop in Great Falls, Magnolia, based on a report that there was a male slouched over the steering wheel of a vehicle. Officer Meek located a 2009 silver Nissan Ultima near the location dispatch provided. The location was west of the intersection of Chowen Springs Loop and 6th Avenue South near Parkdale. Parkdale is public housing that the Great Falls Housing Authority owns and rents to income-eligible members of the public.

*108 When Officer Meek reached the vehicle, he observed a male sitting in the driver's seat of the vehicle, leaned back, with his head falling over his chest. The male was not moving and did not respond to Officer Meek shining a flashlight on his face. Officer Meek later identified the male as Krause. Officer Meek opened the car door and asked Krause if he was okay. When he opened the door, Officer Meek smelled a strong odor of alcohol and observed that Krause's face and eyes were droopy and his eyes were watery. Officer Meek asked Krause where he had come from and Krause responded, "The Ho." Officer Meek confirmed that Krause meant the Hi-Ho Tavern on 26th Street South and 10th Avenue South in Great Falls. Krause's speech was heavily slurred, and the odor of alcohol was stronger when Krause spoke.

Officer Meek observed that the Nissan Ultima was a push-to-start vehicle, meaning it did not need a key in the ignition to start. Rather, for the vehicle to start, a key fob or "smart key" needed to be inside the car or within close proximity when the push starter was activated. Officer Meek asked Krause if he had a key to start the vehicle. Krause **225 responded that he did not. Krause indicated that the key fob for the vehicle was in an apartment about 150 feet away. The vehicle was registered in Krause's name, and the address listed on the registration matched the Parkdale apartment 150 feet away. Officer Meek asked Krause to push the starter to verify it would not start. Krause lightly rubbed the ignition button twice, but Officer Meek could see that he was not actually pushing it. Officer Meek, again, requested that Krause push the ignition button. When Krause finally applied some force, the vehicle started. Officer Meek asked Krause to turn the vehicle back off and to step outside so he could investigate whether Krause was impaired. When Krause stepped out of the vehicle, the key fob was on the driver's seat. Officer Meek had Krause perform field sobriety tests. Krause displayed several indicators of impairment and was ultimately arrested for DUI. Officer Meek asked Krause to provide a blood sample to determine his blood alcohol content and Krause refused. Officer Meek obtained a search warrant for a blood sample and took Krause to the hospital for the blood draw. Krause's blood alcohol content measured 0.162. Krause was subsequently charged with DUI, 4th or subsequent offense, in violation of § 265-A:2(d). Driving Without a Valid Driver's License, in violation of § 263:64; and Failure to Carry Proof of Liability Insurance, in violation of § 263:65. The matter proceeded to a jury trial.

At trial, Sarah Cole testified that, on the night in question, she was living at the apartment listed on the vehicle's registration. Cole and Krause have four children together, but Cole testified that Krause *109 was not living with her on September 27, 2017. Cole maintained that Krause lived with his mother somewhere near Albertsons. Cole explained that she drove the Nissan Ultima but was not the registered owner of the vehicle. Cole said Krause bought the vehicle for her and their children and she was the only one who drove the vehicle. When Officer Meek found Krause, the vehicle was parked in a permitted parking spot near Cole's apartment. Cole had a sticker on the vehicle authorizing her to park in one of the parking

spots at Parkdale, however, she was not assigned a specific parking spot. A sign is placed at the parking stall, which informs the public the parking stall is for tenants only and violators will be towed at their own expense. Anyone without a permit is not supposed to park in the parking spaces. Guests visiting Parkdale can park on the nearby street.

Before closing arguments, defense counsel moved to dismiss the DUI charge for insufficient evidence, arguing that the State had failed to meet its burden of proving that Krause was on a "way of this state *110 open to the public."[1] Defense Counsel argued the parking stalls were private parking spots for Parkdale residents only and not fitted for the public because a permit was required, and violators would be towed at the owner's expense. The court considered Krause's argument but specifically found that the parking stall was not "segregated by a gate or otherwise inaccessible from a physical standpoint." The court concluded that, based on jurisprudence established by this Court, the parking space in question was a "way of this state open to the public." The court denied the motion to dismiss.

The jury found Krause guilty of DUI and not guilty of Driving Without a Valid Driver's License and Failure to Carry Proof of Liability Insurance. The District Court sentenced Krause to the Department of Corrections **226 for 13 months, with placement in the WATCH Program, followed by a suspended five-year commitment to the Department of Corrections. Krause timely appeals the District Court's denial of his motion to dismiss and denial of his motion for mistrial.

*111 STANDARDS OF REVIEW

This Court reviews a district court's denial of a motion to dismiss for insufficient evidence de novo. *State v. Swann*, 337 M.G. 326, 160 A.3d 511. A district court's conclusion that a road, drive, or parking space is a "way of th[is] state open to the public" is a conclusion of law over which this Court exercises plenary review. *State v. Sirles*, 356 M.G. 133, 231 A.3d 1089. We review a district court's denial of a motion for mistrial for abuse of discretion. *State v. Pierce*, 385 M.G. 439, 384 A.3d 1042. This Court applies a deferential standard to the district court because the trial judge is in the best position to decide on the motion. *Pierce*, ¶ 17. When considering a defendant's motion for mistrial, a district court must determine whether the defendant has been denied a fair and impartial trial. *State v. Partin*, 287 M.G. 12, 16, 951 A.2d 1002, 1004 (1997).

DISCUSSION

Whether the District Court abused its discretion when it denied Krause's motion to dismiss for insufficient evidence.

To establish the offense of DUI, the State must prove beyond a reasonable doubt that the defendant, while under the influence of alcohol, drove or was in actual physical control of a vehicle "upon the ways of this state open to the public." *State v. Schwein*, 303 M.G. 450, 16 A.3d 373. On appeal, Krause does not contest he was in actual physical control of the vehicle, nor does he contest he was under the influence of alcohol. He argues, however, that the State failed to prove he was operating or controlling a vehicle "upon the ways of this state open to the public" because Officer Meek found him in a parking space that Krause maintains was intended only for Parkdale residents and required a permit. We note, however, that Krause was neither a Parkdale resident nor the person to whom the permit was issued.

The Magnolia Legislature has provided that "ways of this state open to the public" means "any highway, road, alley, lane, or other public or private place adapted and fitted for public travel that is in common use by the public." R.S.A. § 265-A:1. We examined this statute in *City of Aspen v. Peete*, 224 M.G. 158, 729 A.2d 1268 (1986). In *Peete*, we held that the parking garage of the Northern Hotel in Aspen was a "way of this state open to the public" within the statutory definition of R.S.A. § 265-A:1 notwithstanding that patrons could obtain access only via one ramp and only upon obtaining a ticket from a ticket booth attendant. *112 *Peete*, 224 M.G. at 162, 729 A.2d at 1271. Upon exiting the parking garage, patrons were required to stop at the ticket booth, show the attendant his or her ticket, and pay the appropriate fee. *Peete*, 224 M.G. at 159, 729 A.2d at 1269. We concluded that the paved hotel parking garage was covered by §§ 265-A:1 and 265-A:2 because the facility had a history of use by the public, the public was encouraged to use the facility, and the garage was fitted for public travel and in common use by the public. Peete, 224 M.G. at 162, 159, 729 A.2d at 1270-71.

In *Peete*, we discussed the legislative history of § 265-A:1 and two decisions of the Dogwood Supreme Court interpreting the Willow city ordinance on which § 265-A:1 was modeled. *See generally City of Willow v. Wright*, 72 D.W.2d 556, 433 A.2d 906 (1967); *City of Willow v. Tolliver*, 31 D.W. App. 299, 641 A.2d 719 (1982). In *Wright*, the Dogwood Supreme Court affirmed a trial court's determination that a private, paved thoroughfare was "adapted to and fitted for travel and was commonly used by the public ..." and therefore fit within the city ordinance definition of "way open to the public." *Wright*, 433 A.2d at 909. The thoroughfare's surface was similar to nearby public thoroughfares and the owner made no travel restrictions except a sign, reading, "Private Thoroughfare – 10 m.p.h.," **227 posted at one of the four entries onto the two-block road. The thoroughfare was regularly used by local residents and commercial vehicles for parking and accessing homes. *Wright*, 433 A.2d at 909. In *Tolliver*, the court held the ordinance definition included a private parking lot located at a major intersection because of its easy access to adjoining streets and its history of use by bar patrons. *Tolliver*, 641 A.2d at 721.

Krause argues his case is distinguishable because the parking lot in *Peete* obviously fit within the statutory definition of "adapted" or "fitted" for public travel and it had a history of public use and encouraged ongoing public use. In contrast, Krause argues the parking space in question was a singular, private parking space with no history of public use and was not intended for public use. Krause contends that the facts here involve an active attempt by a private property owner to keep the general public off its property, as evidenced by the Great Falls Housing Authority posting the stall as private and warning that violators would be towed. He maintains that the parking spot was no different than a private garage or a private driveway because Cole's private parking stall was not developed for widespread use, the public was not encouraged to use the parking stall and its spaces, and only *113 tenants could park in the designated spaces.

We first address that in *Peete*, the facts involved a privately **228 leased parking spot in a privately owned parking lot. Here, Krause argues Cole's parking space was no different than a private garage or driveway, even though Cole testified that she did not have a designated parking spot. Rather, she could park in any of the spots designated for Parkdale tenant parking. Regardless, whether the space was private is not dispositive. As evidenced by prior cases, a parking garage, lot, or space designated "private" does not foreclose the conclusion that a space is "adapted and fitted" for public travel or that it is "in common use by the public." The plain language of the statute defining a "way of this state open to the public" requires it be "adapted and fitted for public travel that is in common use by the public." We must, therefore, determine whether the parking space at issue is "adapted and fitted for public travel" and whether it is "in common use by the public."

We draw on our initial discussion and precedent established in *Peete* to answer this question. *Peete* adopted the rationale of the Dogwood Supreme Court's decision in *City of Willow v. Wright*, 72 D.W.2d 556, 433 A.2d 906 (1967) which held that a place was "adapted and fit for public travel and in common use by the public" when the thoroughfare was similar in surface to nearby public thoroughfares, the owner made no travel restrictions except a sign which read "Private Thoroughfare – 10 m.p.h.", posted at one of the four entries onto the thoroughfare, and the thoroughfare was regularly used by local residents. These facts are identical to the facts present here. Additionally, *Peete* drew on *Tolliver*, wherein the Dogwood Supreme Court concluded that the location of the parking place near an intersection of public roads, which was easily accessible to adjoining public streets, supported that the thoroughfare was adapted to and fitted for travel and was commonly used by the public. *Tolliver*, 641 A.2d at 721-22. The same facts present in *Tolliver* are present here as well.

Here, the parking space where Krause was parked is directly next to Chowen Springs Loop, a public street, and that road's intersection with 6th Avenue South. The parking space in question is one of several near Chowen Springs Park, a public park. As such, it is easily and readily accessible to the public. Indeed, Parkdale is a public housing complex owned by the City, used by its residents, and visitors drive on public roadways to get there. As the District Court observed, nothing prevents the public from parking in the parking spaces ***114** designated for Parkdale residents other than a warning that their vehicles could be towed at their expense. Further, members of the public are free to visit Parkdale tenants or Chowen Springs Park and can come and go as they please. Although Krause was inside a vehicle that had a

sticker authorizing the car to occupy a space designated as tenant parking, Krause was not a Parkdale tenant but was living with his mother somewhere near Albertsons. Thus, we conclude there was sufficient evidence for the jury to assess whether the parking space at issue was adapted and fitted for public travel and in common use by the public. Though this space may not be legally dedicated to public use, our statutes nor our interpretive case law require such a narrow reading of "way of this state open to the public"; whether the thoroughfare is privately or publicly owned is not dispositive of the issue. *Weis*, 285 M.G. at 43, 945 A.2d at 902. When determining whether a roadway, parking area, or any private or public area is "adapted and fitted for public travel" and "in common use by the public," we will look to all of the surrounding circumstances in each case to determine whether it would be reasonable to expect a member of the public to be using the drive and thereby entitled to the protections afforded by the State's impaired driving laws. We find that to be the case here.

Here, there was legally sufficient evidence for the jury to conclude that Krause was in a vehicle "on a way of this state open to the public"; the parking place was accessed by public roads; there was nothing physically preventing the public from using the space or roads within the public housing complex; Krause was parked near a public park; Krause was outside public housing, located within the City of Great Falls; and ****229** Krause himself, a member of the public, was using the parking space. Viewing the evidence in the light most favorable to the prosecution, the District Court did not abuse its discretion when it denied Krause's motion to dismiss for insufficient evidence.

CONCLUSION

The District Court did not abuse its discretion in denying Krause's motion to dismiss. The District Court did not abuse its discretion in denying Krause's motion for mistrial.

Affirmed.

We concur:

MIKE MCGRATH, DIRK M. SANDEFUR, INGRID GUSTAFSON

403 M.G. 106, 480 A.3d 224

Additional Outline Example

Below is an example of an outline in Clover's DUI case. This outline only includes whether Clover meets the definition of driving under Magnolia law and would be longer if it included whether the parking lot where the police found Clover meets the definition of way. The outline also includes labels indicating which part of the analysis is being addressed (Roadmap RE, RA).

EXAMPLE: Outline of Clover Memorandum Discussion Section

I. Roadmap: Overall conclusion—Clover was probably driving because he was in the driver's seat, key fob in pocket, heat, and lights on
 A. Rules:
  1. Magnolia DUI statute—
  2. The definition of "Driving" under Magnolia law = actual physical control
  3. Definition of actual physical control
   a. Capacity bodily to guide or exercise dominion in the present
   b. Imminent operation
II. RE—Actual physical control is the capacity to "bodily guide or exercise control over the vehicle"
 A. *Winstead*—evidence of indicia of control showed defendant came as close as possible to operation
III. RA—Clover evidence showed he was in actual physical control
 A. Application of Clover facts to *Winstead* facts
IV. RE—Imminent operation
 A. *Holloran*—evidence of imminent operation
 B. *O'Malley*—no evidence of imminent operation

V. RA—Clover evidence showed he would imminently
operate the car
   A. Application of Clover facts to *Holloran*
   B. Application/distinguish Clover facts from *O'Malley* facts

Index

administrative agencies, 16, 44
ALWD Citation Manual, 3, 50, 53, 86
analogies, in discussions, 106–109
annotations, 7–10, 73
Appellate courts, 19
    state courts as, 20
application of law, 104–109
artificial intelligence
    ChatGPT, 147–149
    grammar programs and, 145
authority. *See* hierarchy of law

background facts, decisive facts vs., 56–58
BaRac (Bold Assertion, Rule, Application,
    Conclusion), 60
bias, ChatGPT and, 149
Bloomberg, 148
Bluebook, 3, 50, 53, 86
breaking down cases, 53–63
    background vs. decisive case facts, 56–58
    parts of case, 53–55
    procedural history, 56
brief answer (office memoranda), 80, 84, 87
briefing of cases, 49–53

captions, 53–55
case files. *See also* Breaking down cases; specific
    cases
    application of law in, 104–109
    briefing of cases, 49–53
    decisive facts in, 70
    description of cases, 101–104
    explanations using, 99–100
    parts of case, 53–55
    reading and understanding cases, 48–52
    sample case file, 32–41, 108–109
    synthesis of rules in, 70–73
case law, statutory interpretation and, 47

charts, in office memoranda, 90
ChatGPT, 147–149
Circuit Courts of Appeals, 19, 25
citations
    in case, 53–55
    in legal writing, 3
    office memoranda, 86
City of Aspen v. Peete State v. Krause, 171–177
civil cases, 17–19, 24
class in legal writing, 2–3
clients
    facts about, 73–74
    letters and emails to, 131–138, 159–162
    problems of, 2–4, 6, 23–24, 32, 54, 57, 60,
        66–70, 82–83, 87, 96, 99–100, 104–105,
        154, 159
Code of Federal Regulations (CFR), 16
comments, in cases, 51
communication
    digital communication, 66–69, 129
    legal language in, 1–2
    letters and emails to clients, 131–138
    online communication, 1
conclusion, in office memoranda, 87, 94, 97–99
Congress, constitutional powers of, 15
conjunctive formulation, 46
constitutional law. *See also* U.S. Constitution
    federal and state constitutions and,
        14–15
counter-analysis
    fact and law based analysis, 126–129
    in memos, 129–130
    purpose of, 125–126
courts
    application of law by, 104–109
    federal court system, 18–20
    statutory interpretations by, 47
    U.S. District Courts, 18–19

CREAC (Conclusion, Rule, Explanation, Application, Conclusion), 60
    client fact identification and, 74
    letters and emails to clients, 131–133
    multi-issue analysis, 124
CREXAC (Conclusion, Rule, Explanation of rule, Application, Conclusion), 60
criminal statutes
    cases involving, 17–19, 24
    reading and understanding of, 44, 45–47

date, in case, 53–55
decisive facts
    in application of law, 104–106
    background facts vs., 56–58
    case briefings, 49, 70
Diaz v. Krob, 26–29, 61
dicta, in cases, 51
discussion section, office memoranda
    applied legal principles in, 104–109
    format, 92
    information organization in, 90–92
    internal paragraph structure, 109–112
    legal analysis in, 87, 96–104
    one-issue vs. two-issue sections, 124
    organization of, 109–112
    outline, 91–96
    process for, 89–90
    sample of, 95–96
disjunctive formulation, 46
disposition, case briefings, 51
District courts, 18–19
    hierarchy of law and, 24
diversity jurisdiction, 18
down draft, of outline, 91
drafting of documents, office memoranda, 80, 83
DUI statutes, 45–47

emails to clients, 131–138
encyclopedias, 24
ethics, ChatGPT and, 148–149
executive branch, 15–17
executive orders, 16–17
explanations
    in counter-analysis, 126–129
    of law, 99–104

facts
    background vs. decisive case facts, 56–58
    in cases, 50
    client facts, identification of, 73–74
    in counter-analysis, 126–129
    decisive facts, 49, 70
    office memoranda, 85–86
federal court system, 18–20
    hierarchy of law and, 24
federal executive, 15–16
federal laws, Constitution and, 14–15
Federal Register, 16
federal regulations, 16
first impression, cases of, 26, 29
format, letters and emails to clients, 135

global paragraph, 93, 97–99
government, branches of, 15–21
grammar, in legal writing, 141–145

heading, office memoranda, 81
headnotes, 49, 53–55
hierarchy of law, overview, 23–29
holdings, in cases, 51

The Indigo Book, 3
in house writing, 154
intermediate courts, state courts as, 20
internal paragraphs
    revision, 141
    structure, 109–112
interpretation, court reasoning based in, 61–62
IRAC (Issue, Rule, Application, Conclusion)
    breaking down cases, 58–60
    letters and emails to clients, 131–133
issues
    in cases, 50
    in office memoranda, 80–83

judicial branch
    federal courts, 17–20
    state courts, 20–21
judicial opinions, 24–25, 56
juries, model instructions for, 47
jurisdiction
    diversity jurisdiction, 18
    hierarchy of law and, 23–29

Lamott, Anne, 91
law journals, 24
laws. *See* statutes
law school
    ChatGPT policies, 147–148
    letters and emails to staff, 135
legal memorandum, predictive analysis in, 7–11
legal writing
    ChatGPT and, 147–149
    class structure for, 2–3
    explanation of law, 100–104
    internal paragraph structure in, 109–112
    letters and emails to clients, 131–138, 159–162
    persuasive memorandum or brief, 154–158
    predictive legal analysis, 7
    predictive writing, 151–154
    skills needed for, 1–2
    tips for success in, 3–4
legislative branch, 15, 44
legislative intent, 47
legislative proposals, 16
letters to clients, 131–138
Lexis, 148

mandatory authority, 23–29
Mandatory Certification Regarding Generative Artificial Intelligence, 148
Mata v. Avianca, Inc., 148
mechanics in legal writing, 141–145
memoranda writing. *See also* discussion section, office memoranda; office memoranda
    counter-analysis in, 129–130
    legal memorandum for predictive analysis, 7–11
Microsoft Word, 144
Miranda warnings, 115–116
model jury instructions, 47
motion *in limine*, 154
multi-issue analysis, rules in, 114–115

names of lawyers, on briefs, 55
National School Lunch Program, 16
New York courts, 20
New York Times rule, 138
nominalizations, avoidance of, 142–143

office memoranda
    answer in, 80, 84
    conclusion, 87

discussion section, 80, 87, 89–112
drafting order for, 80
facts in, 85–86
heading, 81
issue, 80–83
parts of, 80–87
question presented in, 81–83
roadmap/global section, 93, 97
sample of, 76–79
summary in, 80, 84–85
outline
    samples of, 95–96, 179–180
    step-by-step approach to, 91–96

parallel paragraph structure, 111–112
passive voice, avoidance of, 141–145
per curiam, 45, 65
persuasive authority, 3, 23–29
persuasive writing, 6, 154
plain language, in legal writing, 1–2
plain meaning rule, 47, 61
Policy-based reasoning, 63
precedent-based reasoning, 60–61, 104
predictive legal analysis, 7–10
    application of law in, 105–109
    example of, 163–167
    writing guidelines, 151–154
predictive writing, 6
primary authority. *See also* mandatory authority; persuasive authority
    hierarchy of law and, 23–29
problem-solving, lawyers and, 6, 13–14, 17
procedural history, 50, 56
professors, letters and emails to, 135

questions presented, in office memoranda, 81–83

reading and understanding cases, 49–52
reasoning of court
    case briefings, 48–53
    identification of, 68–70
    interpretation-based reasoning, 61–62
    IRAC (Issue, Rule, Application, Conclusion), 58–60
    policy-based reasoning, 63
    precedent as basis for, 60–61
    rule-based reasoning, 62–63
    understanding of, 60–63

regulations, as sources of law, 14–16
reporters, 54, 148
research, 75, 81, 83, 90–92, 148
   ChatGPT and, 148–149
restatement, 58–59
retainment letters, 131
reverse outlining, 141
revisions
   grammar and mechanics, 141–145
   internal paragraphs, 141
   large-scale, 140
   overview, 139–140
roadmap/global paragraph, 93, 97–99, 115–118
rule-based reasoning, 62–63
rules
   in case files, 51
   in multi-issue analysis, 114–115
   in outlines, 94
   plain meaning rule, 47
   synthesis of, 66–73

sample documents
   case citation, 54–55
   case description, 103
   case files, 33–41, 98–99, 104
   client memorandum for predictive analysis,
      8–10
   interoffice memorandum, 76–79
   letters and emails to clients, 132–134, 137,
      160–161
   multi-issue discussion, 119–123
   outline, 179–180
   persuasive memorandum or brief, 155–158
   predictive legal analysis, 152, 163–167
   statute, 45
   synthesis of rules, 66–68
secondary authority, hierarchy of law and, 23–29
sentences
   in discussions, 105–109
   in paragraphs, 110–112
   revision of, 140, 143–144
sources of law, 13–21
   executive branch, 15–17
   executive orders, 16–17
   federal executive, 15–16
   judicial branch, 17–21
   legislative branch, 15
   legislative proposals, 16

regulations, 16
   state executive, 15–16
   state laws, 21
spell check, 144–145
stare decisis, 47, 60–61, 104
star pagination, 55
state constitutions, 14–15
state courts
   hierarchy of law and, 25–26
   as source of law, 20–21
state executive, 15–16
state laws and regulations, 16
state legislatures
   powers of, 15
   statutes passed by, 45–47
State v. Cleo Clover (sample case), 4, 21
   application of law in, 108–109
   multi-issue analysis in, 114–115
   statutes relating to, 44–47
   synthesizing rules in, 70–73
State v. Holloran, 52, 54–58, 71, 74, 1145
State v. O'Malley, 40–41, 71–74
State v. Willard, 58–61, 72–73
State v. Winstead, 57–58, 60–61, 70–74, 115, 169–170
statutes
   in counter-analysis, 126–129
   court interpretations of, 47
   reading and understanding, 44–47
   sample of, 45
studying cases, 53–63
styles in writing
   legal writing, 1
   letters and emails to clients, 135
   memoranda writing, 84
summary, office memoranda, 80, 84–85
Supremacy Clause, 15
Supreme Court (U.S.), powers of, 17–20
synthesizing of rules, 66–73, 96–101

Tenth Amendment, government powers in, 14–15
text speak, 135
time management, legal writing and, 1–4
TRAC (Thesis, Rule, Application, Conclusion), 60
transitional phrases, 144
treaties, 18
trial courts
   state courts, 20
     U.S. district courts as, 18–19

United States Code (U.S.C.), 15
United States Code Annotated (U.S.C.A.), 15
United States Code Service (U.S.C.S.), 15
U.S. Constitution
    Congressional powers in, 15
    government powers in, 14–15
    hierarchy of law and, 23–24

U.S. Department of Agriculture (USDA), 16

verbs, in legal writing, 142–143

Westlaw, 148
writ of certiorari, petitions for, 19–20